HOW TO SEE IN THE SPIRIT

HOW TO SEE IN THE SPIRIT

Michael R. Van Vlymen

HOW TO SEE IN THE SPIRIT

A Practical Guide on Engaging the Spirit Realm

Copyright © 2013 Michael R. Van Vlymen

All rights reserved.

HOW TO SEE IN THE SPIRIT

Dedication

I would like to dedicate this book to the Lord Jesus Christ. Thank You for paying the price, and thank You for your patience with me as you taught me these truths.

I also dedicate this book to my amazing wife, Gordana. Your support, encouragement and love have been invaluable, and this book would not have been otherwise possible.

HOW TO SEE IN THE SPIRIT

Table of Contents

HOW TO SEE IN THE SPIRIT

Acknowledgments

I acknowledge first and foremost, the Lord Jesus Christ, the Father, and Holy Ghost.

To my wife, Gordana, my son Matthew, and daughter Angelina, who are taking this journey with me.

To my parents, Marvin and Cathy, who introduced me to the Lord, and taught me that there is no life apart from Him.

Also, to the many servants of the Lord, who have taught, imparted, prophesied or prayed over my family and I. I honor them for their service and faithfulness to the Lord.

Bobby Conner, Gary Oates, Bob Jones, Jane Hamon, Ryan Wyatt, Joshua Mills, David Hogan, Joe D. Hogan, Mahesh Chavda, Kim Settles, Jeff Jansen, Bill Johnson, Will Hart, Randy Clark, Benny Hinn, Dr. Lester Sumrall, Win Worley, Mel Bond, Dr. Bruce Allen, Sid Roth, Patricia King, Lyn Packer, Paul Keith Davis, John Belt, Neville Johnson, Sadhu Sundar Selvaraj, Curry Blake, Emerson Ferrell, Ana Mendez Ferrell, Jamie Galloway, John Paul Jackson, John Fenn, Kathie Walters and Steven Brooks. Also, to the many others whose instruction, books, and materials have brought great blessing and revelation.

I also want to acknowledge our friends and fellow servants, the angelic host, who have ministered to us and protected us in unwavering faithfulness to the Lord.

Introduction

In the year 2009, the Lord began to open my eyes to the spirit realm. And the Lord began to teach me about the spirit realm, and how to see in the spirit realm through a series of dreams, visions, experiences and visitations. Through these experiences I learned how a person's spiritual sight is gained or lost.

Because of these experiences and what I learned from them, my Christian life took on a vibrancy and depth that I never knew could have ever existed. I had never been so excited about spiritual things and my walk with the Lord.

It was an amazing and exciting time. Because of the impact these revelations had on me, I wanted to share this with others. I began to tell people things the Lord had shown me about spiritual sight and how to engage the realm of the kingdom.

I discovered that there are a lot of hungry people out there! People are hungry for the deep things of God. Hungry to really know God up close and personal.

Early on I had felt that I was supposed to keep an account of all of the experiences and revelations that the Lord was giving me, so I kept a journal. Over the course of the last four years I had compiled several journals. In 2012 I began to ask the Lord if these journals had a greater purpose or were solely for my own record and personal use.

It was only a matter of a few weeks that had gone by, when a friend invited me to an outreach conducted in our city by a Christian Ministry of Dayton Ohio. An anointed Apostle was speaking and I enjoyed his teaching very much.

After the service, I went to the front to tell the Apostle that I had been blessed, and the exchange went something like this.

"Excuse me. I really enjoyed your message tonight. Do you ever pray for people...."

At this point the apostle laid hands on me and began to prophesy.

"Write! Write! Write! Clear off everything from your desk except for your notebook and your Bible and write!"

He also declared several other things that came to pass. I was a bit shocked, to say the least. The Lord had answered, very specifically, the question that I had asked. It left little room for doubt as to what I was supposed to do.

So, for all of you who desire to see the unseen and engage the realm of the kingdom...here it is.

This book is for you.

Foreword

Many Christians are fearful of the supernatural or have been taught that the gifts of the Spirit are not for our generation, but if we are to fulfil the great commission it is important that we overcome this fear which binds us and focus on what is important. I am not usually the type of person to recommend books or CDs lightly, unless they really minister to me first and I have always been wary of "How to books" when it comes to things of the Holy Spirit, but I have to say that this book by Michael Van Vlymen really grabbed my attention. I loved the fact that the emphasis was not only on the supernatural, but also the need to soak oneself in the Word of God, so that we become rooted and grounded in our faith having our head in heaven and our feet firmly planted on the earth.

Smith Wigglesworth a man used mightily by God in the supernatural in the mid 1900's prophesied about a generation to come, that would experience a move of the Spirit where the emphasis would be on "The Word and The Spirit". I believe that we are living in that generation. The message of this book therefore is very timely, and is an excellent resource for those seeking a deeper walk with the Lord, and a hunger to move in the Supernatural. I therefore whole heartedly recommend this book with out hesitation, and pray that you too may be as blessed as I was. I encourage you to take time in seeking the Lord, that he may restore to you what the enemy has stolen. Michael has written a masterpiece, don't miss it...

John Scotland

CHAPTER ONE
Connect to the Power

As we begin this journey, it is important to know that God Himself is helping you. He withholds no good thing from you.

One very important thing I learned was that God will take you as far, and as fast, as you are willing to go. I heard Bobby Conner make that statement several years ago, and to be honest, I doubted it for a couple of years. I thought, there has to be more to it than that. How could our willingness determine to any real degree, what kind of supernatural power or gift, God might grant to us?

I didn't really understand this until I experienced the reality of it through desire. And it made me very aware that The Lord did not make this complicated at all. It is so simple that anyone can enter in, even a child.

Angels are not hiding from you! Jesus isn't out there far away somewhere wondering if you will ever figure it out!

All of Heaven is intimately involved in your life. You are being constantly drawn into a deeper walk with the Lord. He is continuously engaging you, to give you revelation, to open your eyes, to open your ears, so you can hear God's voice.

I am not talking figuratively here. The Lord desires to fellowship with you. The heavenly host are part of your ministry team!

And you are a part of theirs! They are constantly trying to "wake us up!" So as we begin this journey, please keep that in the forefront of your spirit.

ⓘ *Salvation*

The power source is God, and connecting to Him is called salvation, or being born again. For engaging the spirit realm this foundation is critical. First and foremost, you must be born again if you pursue this spiritual reality.

Of course I know that there are many people who can see in the spirit, and do not embrace Jesus as their Savior. They are practicing new age religions and beliefs. The Bible says that they cannot do this legally.

Verily, verily, I say unto you, he that entereth not by the door into the sheepfold, but climbeth up some other way, the same is a thief and a robber. (John 10:1)

New Age

There are many people in the "new age" who operate in the supernatural. Many have been given spiritual gifts by God that the modern day church had no knowledge of or use for.

But let me say this to my new age friends. I know you are thinking, "Why would I trade the supernatural reality I have, to embrace some "religious tradition?" The answer is this. Jesus did not come to earth saying "I'm starting a new religion." Or "I've come to establish religious traditions." What He said was "The Kingdom of Heaven is at hand." And then He backed it up with signs and wonders, *and told His followers to do the same.*

19

I'm very sorry if a Christian family member of mine turned you off to Christ by offering you "religion." The truth is that if you give your life to Him you are moving from the fringes of the supernatural and jumping into the deep end. There is no more powerful supernatural reality than Jesus. He *gave* you the hunger and desire and He wants to bring the fulfillment of it.

All I'm asking you to do is to "taste and see that the Lord is good." Pray the prayer of salvation and *see* if He is telling you the truth.

As believers and heirs of salvation we have divine protection. We have authority given to us by Jesus Christ Himself. There are angelic forces that are responsible for our safety and well being and they take that job very seriously. Non-believers have no such protection and no such authority. I know many people in other religious paths that suffer from attacks of fear and worry and they don't know why. The spiritual atmosphere around them is the reason why.

That is why people involved in sins such as drunkenness and drug use, sometimes see things that terrify them. Certain types of sins lower the spiritual veil and cause people to see the unseen realm. If that person's life is full of ungodliness then that is what they will see around them. And for them it can be terrifying.

If you have a desire to see in the spirit realm but have never made a personal commitment to Jesus, I would encourage you to make that commitment now. Pray this prayer...

"Lord Jesus, Thank you for dying on the cross to pay the penalty for my sins. I ask you to forgive me for all of my sins, and come into my heart right now and be my Savior."

If you meant that, you are now born again! I know it sounds way too simple, but God made it that way for a reason, so that everyone could receive His salvation.

For whosoever shall call upon the name of the Lord, shall be saved.   (Romans 10:13)

The Word

For living as a Christian in general, we are instructed to study and know the Word. In engaging the spirit realm, knowing the Word is even more important for several reasons.

The Word Divides your Soul and Spirit.

For the Word of God is quick, and powerful, and sharper than any two edged sword piercing even to the dividing asunder of soul and spirit, and of the joints and marrow, and is a discerner of the thoughts and intents of the heart. (Hebrews 4:12)

Your spirit man really wants to see the things of God. But, your soul has ties to your spirit and exerts control over it. If your soul is not fully sanctified, it will try to pull you toward the things of the world, and away from the things of God.

We have all heard the saying, (scripture) ...*The spirit is willing but the flesh is weak. (Mark 14:38)*

A common example for many, including me, is when you really *need* to pray, but you are too tired. Your spirit man is telling you to kneel at your bed, and your soul is telling you to climb into it.

Even the disciples faced this very issue and the Lord rebuked them over it.

Then He returned and found the disciples sleeping. "Couldn't you men keep watch with me for one hour?" He asked Peter. (Matthew 26:40)

But the Word is the thing that deals with this issue. By reading and studying and meditating on the Word of God, the Word breaks those ties between your spirit and soul. Then you are able to function more fully as a spirit being and engage your spiritual senses.

Another absolutely huge benefit is that without those soul ties to your spirit, you become more offended at the idea of committing a sin. Your soul is tempted and immediately your spirit is disgusted and shuts down the thought of sinning.

The more you meditate on the Word, the greater the separation becomes and the more your spirit becomes unencumbered with the soul and the flesh. And at this point, actual spiritual veils that cover your eyes begin to be removed.

Your Eyes are washed by the Word.

That He might sanctify and cleanse it, with the washing of water by the Word. (Ephesians 5:26)

The context may be something different, but the fact remains that the Word cleanses and sanctifies.

All the ungodly things we see over the course of a day, even by accident, defile us and our eyes. An angel pointed this out to me one morning as I was praying and waiting on God.

A Visitation

One morning at about 2 a.m., I was praying and waiting on the Lord. Just to see what He might tell me or show me. I looked up for some reason and I could see an Angel of the Lord in the distance. He looked like he was going somewhere, but I called out to him and asked him if he could help me for a minute.

He came over to me and asked, "What can I do for you?" I told him that I wanted to see more clearly. When I told him that, immediately his eyes looked like they were injured and bleeding. I asked him, "What are you doing?" His eyes then became normal again, and that's when he said to me, "Your eyes are damaged from all the garbage you have put into them over the years, but the Lord Jesus can heal them."

And then he turned and left.

Distractions

All the ungodly things we have seen, not only defile us but create distractions that are even more overpowering than the "normal" distractions. The Word of God not only washes and cleanses us, but removes the distractions and our spiritual eyes become more fully capable of seeing. Distractions can be *anything* in the natural that keep us from looking at the spiritual.

What do distractions do? They keep us from seeing in the unseen realm. They keep us focused on, well, the distractions.

Early in my education from the Lord concerning spiritual sight, I would sometimes spend hours trying to see in the spirit. Usually late at night or early in the morning are the time periods I have found to be best for me.

On this particular night, I was laying in the bed in the dark and lying very, very still and quiet. I was looking toward the ceiling and around the room in general. The room had enough light that if I got up I wouldn't trip over anything, but not enough light that I could focus on any of the natural things of my surroundings. (Like dressers and furnature, etc.)

After a short amount of time, perhaps thirty minutes or so, I began to see various very, very subtle shifts in the atmosphere around me. They were things that most people would dismiss as a "trick of the light", or as "your eyes playing tricks on you". (It is something you need to keep in mind from here forward.)

There would be a small flash of light on my left, a movement of some sort on my right and various shifting colors in front of me that I couldn't quite see clearly.

I would focus on the area of movement in a relaxed, yet attentive manner and certain things would become more visible for a moment and then fade from view. It was both exciting and disappointing at the same time. I was excited to see, but I really wanted to see more clearly.

After a while, I said to myself, "I wonder why I can't see any better than this?" About two seconds later I heard a voice say, "Because you are distracted." I actually heard the voice speaking to me in my thoughts, but I was still caught off-guard.

The angel was right, I was distracted. Even though I was trying to see in the spirit, I was looking as if I would see with my natural physical eyes. And that is not correct.

The Word Overpowers Distractions

We live in a natural world. We face issues and problems in the natural world that require us to think along those lines. That's the way it is for all of us, but those natural things don't have to be a distraction. We can focus our attention on natural things *and* be fully engaged spiritually. We do this by meditating on the Word, or by *"Practicing the presence of God."* (Brother Lawrence 1614-1691)

This is accomplished very simply by bringing our attention upon the Word or upon Christ, who is the living Word and when we realize or become aware that we haven't had our focus there, we bring our focus back to that place again.

In my own life even if I am fully engaged in conversation with someone, I can also be aware that the Lord Jesus is there with us. Just in the same way you could be aware if there was another person standing there with you, perhaps listening to your conversation without necessarily talking themselves.

Or if we have chosen a scripture to meditate on for the day, we would keep our focus there and if we need to focus elsewhere, we would then bring our focus back to the scripture as soon as we are able to do so. You don't get condemned over it. You train yourself by constantly doing this until it is first nature.

The Word is your Sword

The Word of God is called the Sword of the Spirit for good reason. It is powerful. It cuts. It is a great weapon.

When your spiritual eyes are opened, you will see a lot of various things in the spirit realm and not all of them are pleasant. It's during those times especially that you realize that the Word is your protection, your defense, your offense and your provision.

I'm sure that you are already aware that demons, devils and other unclean things occupy this realm in the world around us, as well as angels of the Lord. It is far better to plan ahead for this journey, because if you engage the things I talk about in this book, your eyes will be opened and you will need your sword.

You don't want to be in a confrontation *wishing* you could remember the scripture that says you have authority over the enemy.

Please don't be in fear over this though. As Jamie Galloway, Pastor of East Gate Church, West Chester PA says,

"You don't have to be in fear over this. Papa's got love for you. If we ask for bread, He won't give us a stone. If we ask for a fish, He won't give us a scorpion. But we are stewards of our own lives. So, if you go into these realms, know the word.

Everyone knows that even the Lord Jesus himself rebuffed satan using the Word, when tempted by him in the wilderness. In every instance that Jesus was tempted His response was always,...*it is written*...(Matthew 4:1-11)

(3) *The Baptism*

But ye shall receive power, after that the Holy Ghost is come upon you: and ye shall be witnesses unto me both in Jerusalem, and in all Judaea, and in Samaria, and unto the uttermost part of the earth. (Acts 1:8)

The Holy Spirit empowers our Christian life. He gives and empowers very gift, every fruit, and every revelation of Christ. He leads us into all truth, *(John 16:13)*, including the truth of spiritual sight.

As you take this journey into the things unseen, sometimes it's hard to know how to pursue it and how to pray. Sometimes we don't even know what to pray for but the Holy Spirit does. So don't hesitate to yield your tongue to Him and let Him help you.

We don't see the big picture like He does. Defer to Him as much as you can and you will be praying the perfect will of God and praying very productive prayers.

Also, sometimes we have issues that have to be dealt with and the Holy Ghost can bring to our minds any un-confessed sins or show us any blocking or hindering spirit that needs to be dealt with.

He empowers the supernatural part of the Christian life. If you have never received the baptism in the Holy Spirit, ask the Lord to baptize you now. If you do not feel that He has poured out His spirit upon you, go to a church where there are those who have a gift of impartation of the gift of the Holy Ghost and let them lead you into it.

You do not have to be baptized in the Holy Ghost to see in the spirit, but it is needed to walk in power for your entire Christian walk, and that includes in the spirit as well.

The Baptism brings Victory

Several years ago I was praying for someone who was acting odd and obviously had a problem. The Lord impressed upon me to pray for the person in tongues. I started to pray in tongues, and had only been praying for a couple of minutes, when an evil spirit "surfaced" and began speaking through the person.

The power of the Holy Ghost had provoked that spirit into betraying himself and revealing his presence, so that the person had the opportunity to be delivered.

A lot of things you see and experience as your eyes are first opened up, you may not know how to react to. Praying in the Holy Ghost is always a safe way to go in these types of situations.

in tongues

CHAPTER TWO
Wisdom and Understanding

The Bible tells us to get wisdom, and with wisdom get understanding.

Wisdom is the principle thing; therefore get wisdom and with all thy getting, get understanding. (Proverbs 4:7)

You can get the greatest wisdom, from people who see openly in the spirit realm. From those who are where you would like to be. You can get step by step instructions that should make it simple to understand, *but,* if you don't have understanding it will do you little or no good.

This may sound like a no-brainer to you. Of course, you say, you have to understand your instructions. That is what I also thought for too long. I would reach the part of a book that talked about understanding, and I would skim through it so that I could get to the "meat."

All of the pages that talked about how we learn, and how our understanding is formed by our own life experiences, I didn't receive. The section that talked about our environment giving us a basis for understanding words, phrases and concepts, for a long time, were lost on me. I really hope that you are a lot smarter than I was. I found eventually that we have to understand what the instruction means to the one presenting it, if we are to benefit fully from it. Let's see some examples.

What is your Book about Really?

As I began searching for books and instruction to help me as the Lord began to open my eyes, it soon began to dawn on me that not everyone has the same concept of what "see in the spirit" means. Suddenly I had a revelation of what all those previous books had been talking about.

For every book I found that talked about spiritual sight from the perspective I wanted to learn, (where your spiritual eyes *really* open up and you *really* see) I would find fifty books that were talking about something entirely different.

I would go to the Christian book section and see titles such as, "See the Unseen" or "And Their Eyes Were Opened", titles like "Spiritual Sight" or "Eyes to See", only to find out within a page or so, that the book was *really* talking about things like, how to be understanding, or how to interpret scripture or how to have an intellectual understanding of some kind.

It was really kind of disappointing. Not that those books were not good books, but that their titles were misleading to me. That is what happens when you try to explain supernatural things by giving them natural explanations. It's a disappointment.

I also encountered the same thing when I tried to find books on our friends and fellow servants, the angels. Titles such as "The Angels in your Life", would be a book about children and "Entertaining Angels", a book on how to plan parties or entertain people. They were nothing whatsoever to do with the angelic realm.

Ask, and Ye Shall Receive

In this journey to see the unseen, you have to be bold enough to ask questions if you don't understand something. If you were not raised in an atmosphere that embraced the supernatural things of God, you may have to spend a little time playing "catch-up" just to understand the terminology.

This idea of wisdom and understanding also applies equally to concepts and instructions even more so than book titles.

Wait, I Say, Upon the Lord

One of the things I heard early on from everyone who had any degree of spiritual sight, was, you have to "wait on the Lord." As you wait on the Lord, you position yourself to receive from God.

That seemed to make sense to me. I was raised in an evangelical church, I knew about waiting on the Lord. Because at almost every church service I had ever been in, we had waited on the Lord.

At the end of almost every service, the Pastor would give an alter call. During the alter call, people would come forward for salvation or prayer, to receive from God.

After a short lull in the action, the Pastor would say, "Let's just wait on the Lord." So... we would wait on the Lord. Sometimes the piano would also play softly in the background, but waiting on the Lord usually took from two to five minutes. And then the service was over. That was about all of my understanding.

That almost sounds ridiculous I know. But I assure you that less than one month ago, I heard of something that was very similar. Someone was receiving prayer for healing, and since the ill person wasn't healed within a minute or two, a bystander impatiently said that it was taking too long. "If God was going to do something He would have already done it by now."

But I can't throw rocks at that person, because they were just like me, from a few years ago. If you haven't been taught, how can you know?

What exactly, is Worship?

Understanding about worship also lends itself nicely to this type of example.

I heard a joke from a Prophet who said that most people think praise is three fast songs and worship is three slow songs. You may get that idea yourself sometimes. We get so locked into our agenda, that if the Holy Ghost wanted to do something different, it would ruin our whole "worship" service.

I tell you that across the world, there are churches gathering together in true worship to the Lord, and that the presence of God is so thick that people get healed just by being there.

There are places where gemstones fall out of the atmosphere onto the people as the name of Jesus is lifted up. I have been to meetings where this has happened personally.

You must have understanding. If someone who has the gift you desire, tells you that you need to wait more, or you need to pray more or worship more, ask them what they mean by that. Ask them what that looks like to them.

33

Ask them to give you a moment by moment description of what they do and how they do it. If you don't, you may find yourself just doing more of what doesn't work.

If you are really passionate about having your eyes opened, and you should be, make certain of these things. Ask Holy Spirit to be your mentor. If He is your mentor, you will not be spinning your wheels on this journey and wasting your time.

The Holy Ghost will break it all down for you. Sometimes He gives you an experience and then later the explanation. Sometimes He gives you a teaching and later gives you the experience and spiritual understanding. I will give you several examples to show you how that works in real life, and what that looks like for me, as we get into the "nuts and bolts" so to speak.

Wisdom is getting around the people who are where you want to be, and asking them questions until you really get it. The Holy Spirit helps us as we seek wisdom and understanding.

What is *not* wisdom, is listening to people who do not have a passion to go where you want to go, nor are walking in the gifts you desire, but want to tell you that if God wanted you to have it that He would just give it to you. These kinds of instructions are not wisdom. Do not hang around people who denounce and denigrate the supernatural things of God. They will affect the atmosphere around you. It can strip you of whatever strides you have made in your passion and walk. Doubt and unbelief is your sworn enemy. Pastor Bill Johnson calls the people who do not believe in the supernatural power of God, "unbelieving believers".

You can love them, you can pray for them, you can even pray with them, but you cannot drink from their spirit. I am not saying that these people don't love the Lord. I am saying that they are not ready or willing to accept the revelation.

Many people never accept or believe in divine healing until someone they love needs a touch from God. God is merciful and He will meet us where we are at if we are willing.

The Keys of the Kingdom

There is nothing without Christ. All of your anointing, gifts, miracles, healings, spiritual sight, angelic visitations and Heavenly encounters, flow out of your relationship with Jesus. He is the source. He is the Master Key.

Intimacy with Christ

Knowing that Jesus is the Master Key is a step in the right direction. But we have to keep in the forefront of our minds and our spirits that our motives have to be the Lord Himself.

Yes, the miracles are amazing, the healings phenomenal, seeing in the spirit is beyond anything we have experienced of an earthly nature, angelic visitations are more than a blessing, they are beyond description. But......

We cannot and must not pursue the gifts as an end to themselves. No matter how good our reasons might be. Yes, I want to lay hands on the sick and see them healed. Yes I love to see and experience the miraculous things of God. And I love being in the spirit. And I love seeing angels. But all those things have to flow out of our relationship with Him.

The Lord had to teach me this particular lesson as I began to pursue spiritual things. I began to get so excited about the gifts that I spent less of my focus on the giver of the gifts, and we can't do that.

Everybody wants' to be "Friends" with the Rich Kid

The Lord brought to my mind one day, the idea of all the kids in the neighborhood wanting to be "friends" with the rich kid in the neighborhood. We have all seen movies with plotlines like this.

All the other kids really don't like the rich kid at all, they just want to swim in his pool or play with his toys or eat from his fully stocked kitchen, all the delicacies that they themselves could never otherwise have. The rich kid usually finds out at some point in the movie that nobody *really* likes him, and he is heartbroken. He is just being used.

Like the kind of acquaintance who we might be "friendly" with because we like to borrow their jet ski during the summer.

The Lord spoke to me about me just wanting to use His jet ski. I was guilty. I wanted all the goodies like spiritual sight, angelic visitations, miracles, signs and wonders but I was not cultivating my relationship with Him first and foremost.

The Lord told me that He is happy to let me drive His jet ski, but He wants me to desire for us to do these things *together!* He said that I should come to His house because of my desire for Him, to spend time with Him. And not for the things He can give me.

But seek ye first the Kingdom of God and His righteousness, and all these things shall be added unto you. (Matthew 6:33)

Make sure of your motives, or you can easily open doors to the devil. The devil would be happy to give you experiences in the supernatural realm (apart) from Jesus or a relationship with Jesus. Wrong motives can do just that. An angel of the Lord told me so.....

Jesus to Mike, Your Flight has been Cancelled

I am going to have to reveal some of my failings along the way if I am to give you the benefit of the things I've learned. This next story is exactly that.

Early on in my hunger for spiritual things, I learned that through focus and desire, you can enter into the realm of the spirit. I also learned that in the realm of the spirit, almost anything is possible. In that realm we are not limited to only the things our natural bodies can do.

I discovered that it is possible to fly in the spirit. And boy did I ever love to fly. And so I did

As a matter of fact, that became my mission, so to speak. Every time I found myself in the spirit, either by "accident" or by choice, the first thing I would do is fly. No, the only thing I would do was to fly. I did not go into the spirit to pray. I did not go in to worship. I did not go in for fellowship with the Lord. I just wanted to fly.

Angelic Encounter

On this particular day, I lay down on my bed and purposed in my heart to go beyond the veil. I shifted my focus off of earthly things, and began to focus on moving into the spirit.

After a short time, perhaps thirty minutes or so, it happened, I "shifted" into that realm. So I was now sitting on the edge of my bed, in the spirit, and thrilled to death because I just know I am about to take flight!

But all of the sudden, an angel blasts into the room. He was armored up like a warrior, and I could literally feel an intense power coming off of him. Instantly I was in shock. His gaze was quite fierce, and to be honest, he looked like he was angry with me. When he looked me in the eye, my eyes were locked onto his. Then he told me in a very authoritative voice...

"Quit seeking the supernatural to amuse yourself! You'll open a door to the spirit of witchcraft!"

Then, as powerfully as he came, he left. It was as if a tornado had struck. The entire encounter with this angel was mere seconds, but because of the raw power of God on him, and the speed of the encounter, I felt like I had just been hit by a speeding train.

The Lord had corrected me. I repented.

I am not saying that the life in the realm of the Kingdom can't be exciting. It is! There is a full range of experiences with the Lord and they are exciting! But, it must always flow out of our relationship with Him.

HOW TO SEE IN THE SPIRIT

CHAPTER THREE
The Spirit Realm

The spirit realm is the superior realm that we live in. The seen realm was created from the unseen realm.

By faith we understand that the worlds were framed by the Word of God, so that the things which are seen were not made of things which are visible. (Hebrews 11:3)

It is a little strange to think of something solid and seen, being created out of something unseen. But unseen does not mean unreal. Before you experience the unseen realm, it's hard to get a good grasp on that reality. After you have seen, and or experienced the unseen realm you get it completely.

Also, we need to be or become aware that we do live in both realms. Whether we are cognizant of it or not, it is a reality. The Bible says that *...we are seated in Heavenly places in Christ. (Ephesians 2:6)* We have to understand these scriptures in a different way. We need to understand them in a way that acknowledges supernatural things as *being* supernatural.

The spirit realm is more solid than this physical realm because the physical realm is temporal, fleeting, and in decay.

Engaging the Spirit Realm

You and I engage the spirit realm continually all throughout our days and nights. Every time you pray, every time you worship, and every time you even think or meditate. That is why we are taught in the Word to guard our thought life.

...casting down imaginations.. (2 Corinthians 10:5)

And *...Gird up the loins of your mind...* (1 Peter 1:13)

Thought is the communication mode of the spirit realm. That is how angels can minister to us and devils can tempt us. When you are tempted with an ungodly thought, it is not a random thing. Demons will speak to your mind to make you believe the thought is your own. They will speak to you in "first person."

For example, you may suddenly think, "I sure don't like so and so." Now, if you could see the spirit saying that to you, you would rebuke him and tell him to go away. But, since we don't see them for the most part, we accept the thought as being our own and either reject the thought if we are submitted to Christ, or accept it if we are being carnal.

Every time we pray we make ripples in the spirit realm. We can move Heaven and Earth through the authority of Christ by speaking and declaring His Word.

To more fully engage the spirit realm, and see in the spirit realm, we have to be continually aware that there are unseen things going on all around us at any given time.

We train our senses. We make a *decision* to be aware, to notice things that most people don't. As we do that, the things that

41

appear so fragile and fleeting, open up more fully. Then we begin to see just how substantial those things *really* are.

Beings in the Spirit Realm

There are all kinds of beings in the spirit realm that you may encounter. Of course there are many types and classes of angels, there are living creatures, saints, men in white linen, prophets, and members of the cloud of witnesses.

There are things that I have seen, that are objects in the physical realm, but in the spirit they are alive and have personalities. Everything is alive in Heavenly realms. Everything in Heaven sings praises to God! Even things like rocks.

It all seems very weird at first, but it is a different reality. It is a heavenly reality.

Dark Things

There are also demons and ungodly creatures in the spirit realm. I honestly do not have enough understanding and revelation to know exactly what they are. I just know that they are not good. And the great thing about having the Holy Spirit is that you have a knowing of what is of God and what is not.

There are demons that look as we would expect them to look and others that look beautiful. There are beings that I would describe as having the appearance of tormented souls.

There are people, such as witches and others, who travel into the spirit realm without the blessing of Heaven.

Spiritual Places

I have also seen and experienced demonic places, such as regions of captivity, like jail cells or prisons. In the Psalms, David talks about such places. Until you have actually seen these places, you may think that he is just using his vivid imagination to be descriptive about a low time in his life.

Bring my soul out of prison, that I may praise thy name: The righteous shall compass me about; for thou shalt deal bountifully with me. (Psalm 142:7)

I experienced these regions of captivity long before I knew what they were or anything about them. After almost a year, the Lord led me to a book by Ana Mendez Ferrell called "Regions of Captivity", and she described and explained in great detail the things that I had experienced firsthand. I highly recommend the book, especially for anyone involved in the deliverance ministry.

Out of the Dungeon

The very first experience I had with the regions of captivity was a great revelation and deliverance that the Lord gave to me.

Here is a little back story to this encounter.

For some time, perhaps a year or more, I had been feeling a distance emotionally between me and my wife and daughter. I could not come up with a logical reason why.

I loved them both dearly and wanted a close relationship with them. But there was something, a coldness of some kind. There was something that kept me from feeling that closeness.

One night I woke up in the middle of the night to find myself in a small enclosure like a prison cell. I want to stress to you that this was not a bad dream. I was wide awake with all my faculties. The bars of the cell and the door of the cell were on fire. Iron bars on fire. As freaked out as I was by this, the Lord gave me the presence of mind to use the name of Jesus.

I stood close to the flaming door and struck at the door twice, *as if* I had a sword. I shouted "Fall in the name of Jesus!" twice also. The door fell and I walked out of the cell, up a long stairway out of a deep place, through a doorway and into the light. I immediately saw my wife and daughter, and they had a beautiful glowing countenance.

The next day my relationship with them was completely restored. I felt warm and loving toward them and had no trouble showing them love and affection. Complete deliverance from whatever bondage I had been under. It was amazing!

Heavenly Places

I know that there are many beautiful and wonderful heavenly places as well, but I have personally only experienced a few of the heavenly places, and very briefly.

Also in the spirit, the heavens and the stars and solar systems are places you may see.

The Spirit realm is so vast that I could not really do justice to describing it. Your adventure into the realm of the spirit and spiritual sight in general will be a continuous unfolding, seemingly without end.

Movement in the Spirit Realm

There are no constraints in the spirit like we have in the natural realm. Time and distance are not laws there. Time exists *in* God, and it is not unusual to move forward or backward in time as the Lord sees fit.

Also, distance likewise does not present any obstacle for us. We can move at the speed of thought in the spirit. We can go anywhere in a moment. We can go to the stars and galaxies, to other planets, to places across the face of the earth. And of course we can go to heavenly places as well.

I have heard numerous testimonies of people moving through time and across vast distances to preach the Gospel, or for other purposes the Lord has.

I have personally experienced this on numerous occasions, as have some of my friends and at least one of my family members. I believe God is doing these types of things to train us for the days to come. The following account shows me that God is moving us ahead a little bit at a time.

Movement for Ministry

I received a call not too long ago from one of my family. Her first words were something like "You are not going to believe what just happened!"

I was excited already! She proceeded to tell me of how while driving home from work, taking the route she always takes, turning left here and then right there and then down the main road.

45

She went down a slight hill that she had been down many, many times on her way home, when suddenly she found herself on a different road, one that was ten miles away. It was impossible. Yet God had moved her in a moment to another location, car and all!

On top of all that, the Lord also gave her supernatural vision for the rest of the new route home. (Where you can see close and far away at the same time) She was in awe to say the least, and I was too! God was teaching her something. Be teachable!

Lessons in the Spirit

This was not the first time she had experienced supernatural things. Previously, she had seen in the spirit, an evil spirit. Then, she had traveled in the spirit to another person's home, where she encountered and rebuked and drove out an evil spirit. Then, there were a few other lessons the Lord took her through. And then, of course, there was the supernatural transportation episode.

I believe the Lord is taking her, as well as many, many others through a series of learning experiences to move in the spirit, and move in the power of God.

When your spiritual eyes are opened, you can expect for the Lord to use you in many unusual ways, *if you are willing.*

What does all this have to do with seeing in the spirit? Well, seeing in the spirit is not a "static" thing. It is not an event unto itself, but a doorway if you will, to the spirit realm itself.

That is why all the knowledge and preparation is so important as you move into the spirit. You will need to have some understanding so that you are not completely thrown by what you see and experience. You will have presence of mind to interact with the angels or receive the message they are trying to deliver, instead of staring at them with your mouth open for the first couple of years. (Yes, I was guilty)

Is this Really for Us?

I have heard some ask, "Where are those things in the Bible?" Good question. All throughout the Bible is my answer. From Genesis forward, there are astounding spiritual experiences all the way to Revelation.

Just remember, we have ample precedent to experience being in the spirit or experiencing spiritual sight. Just like John for example.

I was in the spirit on the Lord's day, and heard behind me a great voice... (Revelation 1:10)

You however, are not in the realm of the flesh but in the realm of the spirit, if indeed the Spirit of God lives in you. And if anyone does not have the spirit of Christ, they do not belong to Christ. (Romans 8:9)

I know a man in Christ who fourteen years ago was caught up to the third heaven. Whether it was in the body or out of the body, I do not know- God knows. And I know that this man- whether in the body or apart from the body, I do not know but God knows- was caught up to paradise. He heard inexpressible things, things that man is not permitted to tell. (2 Corinthians 12:2-4)

And Elisha prayed, "Oh Lord, open his eyes so he may see"... (2 Kings 6:17)

There is ample precedent to pursue spiritual gifts and spiritual things. All through scripture, God's people have been doing radical things for God, interacting with angels, going into the heavens, doing the miraculous, etc.

It makes no sense that we would be the only ones exempt. It is plain wrong to believe that we would be the only generations who are not required to fulfill the mandate that Matthew ten talks about, and the greater works.

Just depend on the Holy Spirit to teach you and lead you into all truth. Stay close to the Lord and He will direct your path. He will protect you and amaze you and bless you! It really is a grand adventure that has to be experienced to be believed.

HOW TO SEE IN THE SPIRIT

CHAPTER FOUR
Focus and Awareness

One night I woke up and decided to pray for a little while. I just continued to lie in bed and began to engage the Lord in conversation. After a little while, I began to talk to the Lord about one of my favorite subjects, seeing in the spirit.

The conversation between us was not at all strained and I wasn't interceding or anything at all like that. It was more like two friends just hanging out talking about stuff. It was very relaxed and seemed completely natural to me.

I had heard previously from many others that there are lots of ways to see in the spirit. People like Bob Jones, and Ryan Wyatt and others whom I respect. I didn't really have a lot of understanding about it though, because I didn't have a lot of experience with it.

So I was asking the Lord to explain to me how we actually see in the spirit and to give me understanding about these things. I soon began to realize that understanding is one of the things that the Lord uses to remove the veils from our eyes. The phrase "I see what you're talking about", is a picture of that. When we understand, we see, more literally than we are aware.

So Many Ways to See

The Lord responded to me by asking me to open my eyes so He could show me something. I'm going to take you through the experience step by step because it was significant for me.

I opened my eyes and I could see everything natural around me, just like normal. Then He said "Now close your eyes." So I closed my eyes and when I did I could see the spirit realm around me. Again He said "Open your eyes." And this time I could see both the natural and spiritual at the same time, layered together. When I closed my eyes again, I could still see both realms.

The Lord took me through this process about eight times of opening and closing my eyes. Each time there was something different about the way I saw   I could see the natural with my eyes opened or closed. I could also see the spirit realm with my eyes opened or closed.

I could see both with my eyes opened or closed. It was an amazing experience!

The Lord told me that I can see in any way He chooses. He is not limited by what I think the guidelines are. There are no "rules" for Him to follow.

He also made me very aware that He was showing me things about spiritual sight in a way so that I could relate it to natural laws of sight, to make it easy for me to understand. There was far more available!

What it Looks Like

Visions that I have seen in the spirit have been in full color plus. The experience of seeing something but not necessarily interacting with what you see is what I would call a vision.

The reason I say full color plus, is because anything you see in the spirit realm is literally alive. Many times the colors are colors you can't describe completely because they are so different, so vibrant.

Visions have, so far, only happened to me as I have been sleeping. I would wake up suddenly to find myself in another dimension or another place. I would feel the atmosphere around me. I would operate with all my senses, just like you would in the natural realm.

With all of your senses heightened, you experience everything differently.

In one of the visions I had, I went into a kind of portrait gallery. The colors of the portraits were vibrant and amazing and you could "feel" the spirit of the portrait. The portraits appeared to be alive and semi-motionless as if captured in a moment of time, much like a DVD that plays a little snippet, as it waits for you to select "play."

Dreams

Dreams are much the same as visions, in my opinion, in that they can likewise have a life and intensity of color in them. Dreams are a little more elusive to figure out also.

Visions tend to have a pretty solid message or theme to them and dreams, not so much. In my own dreams they can be all over the place or be like a scene being played out in a very straight forward manner.

It's All Just a Dream

Before I had any understanding about this subject, everything was a "dream." It didn't matter what the experience really was, I would always believe it was some kind of dream. If I had a vision, it would be "Wow, I had a real lifelike dream!" or a visitation from an angel, it would be "I saw an angel in my dream last night."

You get the idea. If the only tool you have is a hammer, then every problem looks like a nail. The same goes for understanding these types of things. As you record the things you experience you will begin to notice subtle differences in them. And then you'll notice, not so subtle differences.

That is something to keep in mind as you move forward in your spiritual sight. You are experiencing more now than you know and realize. As you allow yourself to become aware, you will begin to understand them.

Colors and Intensity

For me personally, the things I see in the spirit while I am awake look semi-transparent. They are usually white or light blue. However, the more I *focus* on what I'm looking at, I find the intensity of color and substance increases.

Seeing Orbs while Driving

Several times while driving around, whether on my way to work or other places, I have seen orbs of light. Sometimes they are positioned over cars in traffic, usually very close to, or above the person in the car.

They have been various colors. There was a peach colored orb above a woman who was driving in front of me one day. There was also a huge golden-yellowish orb that I saw move through an intersection in front of me while I was stopped at the traffic light. It was by itself, no human close by.

I mentioned that focus can bring about a clearer manifestation of what you are seeing, and this is true of the orbs in traffic as well. The problem with that is, you can't focus on the unseen too well while you are driving. It's just not a very good idea.

That being said, I was stopped at a light one day on the way home from work, and I looked up above the traffic light for some reason and saw a barely visible orb of blue light. Or, rather what I thought *might* be an orb. (You just never know until you begin to pay attention)

I was about to just ignore it and move on, but decided to focus for just a moment to see if anything happened. As I began to look at the orb, it began to grow in the intensity of color until it almost appeared as a solid ball hanging in mid-air. I would have missed it had I not given it just a fraction of my time.

It All has a Point

In and of itself, what is the benefit from seeing a few supernatural orbs of light floating around? Why is that important? The importance is the acknowledgement. If you realize that things unseen are around you, and you begin to see them more clearly, then the important things will also become clearer.

Many would love for everything from God to be sovereign. But that is not always the case. As you begin to notice and make yourself aware of shifts in color around you, or shifts of light or the atmosphere, it breaks it open in your life. It develops for you.

It is crucial that you honor the little things, the little strides you make as you go along. You will then be in position to receive greater.

As we begin to move into practical application, be very aware of every improvement, everything that your senses pick up helps you develop greater capacity.

CHAPTER FIVE
What is blocking your Sight?

As the Lord began to unpack this for me, He allowed me to experience and see for myself exactly what was keeping me from seeing in the spirit. These things that I mention are by no means exhaustive. There are lots of things that may affect our sight, but the important thing is that the Lord has complete understanding in these matters and He will help you.

The primary things that I discovered in my own experience were veils, scales, demonic devices and devils. Those are the things that I have encountered that inhibit spiritual sight.

Veils

Early on in 2010, The Lord gave me a lengthy lesson concerning spiritual veils. It was early in the morning, perhaps two or three a.m. when the Lord opened my eyes to see the veils.

I had been praying earlier in the night, sitting downstairs in my "prayer chair". Basically praying, worshipping and waiting on God. After a while I went upstairs to bed. But when I go to bed, I don't just fall asleep. I usually try to stay awake for at least a few minutes in case the Lord may still want to speak to me or show me something. I always try to stay hopeful that the Lord in His love for me will bless me with always a little more of His presence and revelation.

As I lay in bed looking up at the ceiling, I was asking the Lord to show me something. Or teach me something. My spiritual eyes were opened and I saw veils hanging in front of me and all around me.

The veils themselves were dark and semi-transparent, but not to a great degree. They looked like curtains or drapes, layered in many layers. It was almost to the point that it would be almost impossible to see anything in that realm because of them.

However, they were not completely opaque and they also had many, many holes and tears and cuts in them. It was like they were not such an impenetrable obstacle after all.

With all these veils covering the spirit realm from my sight, I asked the Lord why it is that sometimes I can see things and why were some of the things I see seemingly so random and odd, like a hand or a man's chest, or the neck of someone's shirt.

The Lord showed me that the veils are constantly moving, and that makes it even more difficult to see through them. . But because the veils are moving, and because they have cuts and holes in them, some quite large, the holes quite often "line up" with each other and the result is that you can see through those holes into the spirit realm.

That's why sometimes we see things that don't make sense to us. If there is an angel standing before us when the holes in the veils line up, we may only see a small part of him for an instant before the veils shift position again.

Three T-Shirts

One evening I was in my bedroom waiting on the Lord, when I looked up towards the end of the bed. There, at about six or seven feet up in the air was what looked like a partial chest, neck and shoulder hanging in mid-air wearing what looked like three t-shirts.

I studied the sight for a few moments, and then asked *myself,* "What in the world is that?" Then someone responded to my question by answering, "That's my tunic."

I have to admit it, sometimes I'm a little slow, but I realized then that I was seeing part of an angel, and it was his voice I heard. As I began to focus on what I *could* see, my sight began to improve and in less than a minute, I could see him standing there. He had an appearance that was light in color and transparent, and had a very pleasant demeanor.

This experience, coupled with my previous instruction from the Lord, showed me that when we focus on what we see in the spirit, it is a "tool" that gets us past the veils.

What removes the veils? What puts all those holes and cuts and tears in them? Well, there is quite a list that is covered in an upcoming chapter but for starters I will tell you that it's things like repentance, forgiveness, sanctification and warfare.

It really isn't difficult, it's just hard. To remove the veils when we've spent years, allowing them to cover us through sin, doubt, ignorance and other things, takes a commitment of our time.

Scales

The scales are completely different in appearance. I saw the scales that block our sight, in a similar way. However I did not get any clear instruction from the Lord on them.

I'm not saying that He didn't tell me. I possibly just didn't hear Him. I have realized something significant over the last few years. And that is this, when you spend years or even most of your life being unaware of God's voice, you have a time of "adjustment" it seems, to hear Him consistently.

The scales seem to be very large, moving and looked to be alive. At least that was the impression I had when I saw them. The scales I saw were eight –sided with some sort of fringe all around them. I actually drew a picture of them in my journal that looked pretty close. They looked similar to this, in appearance.

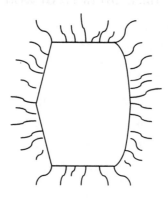

They appeared to be very dense and looked even more difficult to see through.

The scriptures talk about the scales that block our sight. In Acts 9:18 it speaks of *something like scales* falling from Saul's eyes and then he could see.

And immediately there fell from his eyes, as it had been scales: and he received sight forthwith, and arose, and was baptized. (Acts 9:18)

For a long time I thought of these scales as rhetorical, but of course I no longer do.

Demonic Devices

Above all, taking the shield of faith, wherewith ye shall be able to quench all the fiery darts of the wicked (Ephesians 6:16)

In the scripture it talks about weapons of our warfare and the fiery darts of the wicked. David also talks about those that *bend their bows to shoot their arrows*, in Psalm chapter 64.

Of course once you engage the spirit realm, you know that all of these types of things are real. They are real spiritual weapons in the realm of the spirit.

Taken by Surprise

I've already given you one example of demonic "device", and that was the region of captivity I mentioned in chapter three. Another example is the time I woke up in the spirit and as soon as I realized it, I noticed I was in a heavenly place.

It looked like I was about to enter a beautiful heavenly garden of some sort, with beautiful, lush green trees and rolling hills of perfectly manicured grass.

I could see a wonderful park ahead of me, when all of the sudden, someone behind me slipped a hood of some sort over my head and that abruptly ended my experience. (A device)

Stay Close to the Lord

Another time I was in a vision of some sort and I was amazed at how alive and clear my vision and spiritual senses were. In this vision, I happened upon Prophet Bob Jones who was sitting beside a country road in North Carolina adjusting one of his tennis shoes.

I walked over to Bob and asked him, "How long do you have to wait for prophetic revelation?" And his answer to me was, "Until it comes."

As I stood there close to him, my sight was beyond clear, it was amazing, and I realized that. But for some unknown reason I didn't *want* to wait, I wanted to go "explore' the surrounding area. So I began walking away, down a small path, and into the woods nearby. As I got further away, there began to cover my eyes, iron masks, first one then another until I could not really see at all, and was then stumbling along. It was not a pleasant feeling.

The Lord taught me through this encounter, that prophetic revelation brings clear spiritual sight. If I wait upon the Lord, my eyes are opened. That is literally true as well as figuratively

But if I want to pursue my own thing, or my own way or direction, I allow myself to be unprotected. If I'm close to the Lord, I'm ok.

The encounter showed me that following after the flesh, even if it doesn't seem like sin or ungodliness allows the demonic devices to afflict us. Whereas seeking God's plan and will keeps us safe and allows us to operate in the spirit realm as children of God, unhindered and unmolested.

Devils

The devil has no desire whatsoever for us to see in the spirit. It is a lot harder for evil spirits to deceive you or manipulate you if you can see them as they seek to influence you.

Demonic Manipulation

They will do whatever they can to keep your eyes closed. This includes speaking to you, or telling others to speak to you, or speaking through others to you, etc.

What do they say? They talk to you about fear. *"Oh I wouldn't go seeking that stuff if I were you, because all supernatural is of the devil."* Or *"If your eyes are open, you may see things that are really scary and then you won't be able to do anything about it."* They will take anything from your life that has ever caused you to be afraid, and pervert that into a reason as to why you should remain spiritually blind.

They will also get religious on you. Yes, devils really know how to be religious.

They will get your friends and family members to threaten you. (In Christian love of course) They will ostracize you or your family, and break fellowship with you until you repent and fall back into line with them and *"the way we've always done it."*

Everything that has ever been said to you about what "normal" religion should be, they will remind you of in any way they can. And normal does not include seeing in the spirit realm.

This is a very powerful trick of the enemy because *most* people do not want to offend or lose their friends, and they will offend the Lord rather than do that. Sorry, but that is true.

Direct Confrontation

When I first began to learn about deliverance, I found out that devils will try to confront you to back you down. If they can't get you to stop your quest, through the people around you, or if you refuse to listen to them when they try to talk to your mind, sometimes they will get more obvious. They want you to be afraid to see.

Glaring Devils

For two weeks I had been interceding for a young man who was bound by a spirit of lust. On this day, I was in my room "doing warfare.' I was using the authority we have to bind and loose. I had been binding the spirits every day to keep them from doing their evil work so the young man could choose freedom.

I had been praying for perhaps an hour when suddenly two of these demonic spirits appeared in the corner of my bedroom. They stood there glaring at me as if to intimidate me.

By God's grace, I had perfect peace. I continued praying and stared right back at them as I prayed. After a little while they left. As you are contending for your sight, it is not beyond the realm of possibility that this could happen. Don't be intimidated

Bulls of Bashan

Sometimes the devils will be directly opposing your sight and you won't even know it. The Holy Spirit will show them to you so you can deal with it.

It was past ten pm and I had gone upstairs to get ready for bed. I put on my pajamas and went and sat down on the bed to pray my "time to go to bed prayers." I was praying for everybody, with no special request, just a general God bless us and give us good sleep type of prayer.

Suddenly I got the sense I should look up. (The Holy Spirit I'm sure) and standing across the room by the hallway door was some demonic looking thing, that was about seven or eight feet tall, with big horns like a bull. He looked like a dark, wicked man with horns. Again, just standing there looking at me.

I had no idea what it was or how it got in my house, but I knew it was demonic and I began to rebuke it every way I knew how, and was commanding it to leave in Jesus' name.

After about twenty minutes the thing flew away. He had done nothing more than stand there and block the doorway, but it took twenty minutes to drive it out.

Blocking more than the door

Immediately after he left, the space behind him illuminated and one of the most spectacular visions I have ever seen opened up. It was a full, vibrant, living vision that spoke to me about the destiny of my family. It was beyond awesome!

The demon was blocking my *vision*. The Lord wanted me to see something but this thing was preventing me from seeing somehow. He blocked my sight.

The devil does not want you to see anything. He doesn't want you to see your destiny or your provision or your Father's Kingdom, and he will oppose you. Sometimes he will oppose you directly and sometimes indirectly, but he will oppose you. Just remember that the Lord Jesus Christ, King of Kings and Lord of Lords is your defender and your salvation.

Nay, in all these things we are more than conquerors through Him that loves us. (Romans 8:37)

But God hath not given us a spirit of fear, but of power, and of love, and of a sound mind. (2 Timothy 1:7)

It's all Good

So these are the types of things we are contending with. If you are in the spirit interceding against lust, drunkenness, fear, addictions or any other destructive thing, you may at some point face them. But God's grace is enough to deal with it. God has a plan and He will bring it to pass. Do not be discouraged. The victories that the Lord leads you through will increase you, to build you up as sons. (and daughters) Then He will use you to help others win victories as well! It's a great thing!

CHAPTER SIX

Busting through

The Lord has given us everything we need to get us where He wants us to go. That includes recovering our sight. I say recovering our sight because children usually have no or very little trouble seeing into the spirit realm. At one time you probably saw in the spirit just fine.

What happens is, as we get older, we learn such things as doubt and unbelief. We get told over and over, *"It's not real, its' just your imagination."* Then, as we go through life, we see things that defile our eyes and injure them. Add all that up and before you know it we are spiritually blind.

Because most, if not all of our "tools" to recover our sight work in concert with each other, some of the areas we talk about will overlap. I prefer to allow this rather than keep them separate so I can give a full explanation.

Revelation

The Lord loves it when we "get it." Revelation is not just something the Lord gives to us it's something we have to receive as well. It begins to happen when we allow ourselves to think from Heaven's perspective and not our own. How is the Lord honored by what we are seeking or what we are thinking? If we consider the Lord, revelation can engage us.

Bobby Conner's Great Story

I love Bobby Conner. He is one of my favorite people in the world. He also sees in the spirit and has lots of great stories that He tells in order to teach us lessons

Bobby tells a story of being out on the road ministering and preaching and going back to his hotel at the end of the day. He was weary and his feet were tired and sore. As he laid there in the bed, he was thinking about how nice it would be to have a foot massage. So, he said *"It sure would be nice to have someone rub my feet right now."*

He says, all of the sudden the covers flew up to expose his feet and someone grabbed his feet and started rubbing. Bobby says *"I screamed like a little girl!"* and then he yelled *"What are you doing"* and the angel (it was an angel) yelled back *"I'm ministering to you!"*

Well, after I heard that story, I began to tell the Lord "It sure would be nice for an angel to rub my feet." I know that that is probably a real inappropriate thing to be asking the Lord for, for many reasons. But that's what I did. I did that for *two years*! I'm glad God is merciful!

One night about midnight, everyone was asleep and I went to my prayer chair to pray for a while, and this thought came into my head about asking the Lord for an angel to rub my feet. Immediately, an image popped into my head. It was an image that corrected my thinking. It was an image revelation.

As I sat there in my chair, an image of the Lord having spiked driven through His feet came into my mind and I was cut to the heart. I came to my senses. I said "Lord I am so sorry. I should be rubbing your feet instead of asking for a foot rub."

In my mind, I imagined what it would be like to minister to the Lords feet. I imagined massaging His pierced feet because if anyone deserves a foot massage, it's Him.

As this revelation swept over me, I felt an urge to open my eyes and look. As I did, I saw an angel of the Lord there by my feet, holding my left foot in his hands. He wasn't rubbing my foot, he was just holding it. But that foot had had pain in it when I walked, for five or six months, and that pain was instantly gone and has never returned.

That was an important lesson for me, and also for you as well. Revelation opens your eyes.

I spend more time asking the Lord now about what He wants to tell me or show me and less about getting foot rubs. Ask the Lord for the Spirit of Wisdom and Revelation to come upon you.

Repentance

The first thing about repentance is the obvious thing. If you have any sin in your life you have to repent. Turn and go the other way. Get extreme. Repent for yourself, your family, your household, and your ancestors. Leave no stone, as they say.

The previous story could well represent repentance as well as revelation. Repentance breaks legal holds the enemy has over your life to afflict you and that would include your ability to see as well.

Un-confessed sins are one of the arguments demons give as to why they cannot be cast out from their victims during deliverance. Do not allow them to have anything in you that would influence or affect you in any way.

Hereafter, I will not talk much with you: For the prince of this world cometh and hath nothing in me. (John 14:30)

Be like the Lord Jesus and allow satan to have nothing in you!

More Angels than Squirrels

There is a radio comedian that sometimes tells humorous stories. Whenever he has to quantify something in his stories, he'll use squirrels as his measure. For example, in one public interest story, a town in the far north was complaining about being over-run by moose. As he relayed this he said, "There were more moose than squirrels."

I thought it was funny, and began saying of our home, "There are more angels here than squirrels." I thought it was clever. The more I said it, the worse it began to sound to me. I started thinking that perhaps I was being disrespectful of the angelic host or the Lord, or both. One morning as I was getting ready for work, I was just about to walk out the door and began thinking about the angelic presence in our home.

So again I said, "There are more angels here than squirrels." I still wasn't sure, but I thought that if what I'm saying is wrong, why take the chance. So I repented. I told the Lord "I'm sorry. I don't want to be disrespectful. I won't say that anymore."

The Lord has a Sense of Humor

I walked out of the house toward my work truck. I looked to my left and across the yard, I saw a squirrel run into our yard and jump up on our fire pit. He then began to chatter loudly and soon two other squirrels joined him.

These three squirrels then began to run all over our yard making all kinds of racket and within thirty to forty-five seconds squirrels from every surrounding yard and from every direction ran into our yard and began running up and down the slide and play structure, and jumping off of the fire pit and chasing each other all over the yard. It was surreal! I tried best as I could to count them and came up with well over twenty!

The Lord loves it when we repent. And He is not sitting off in the sky somewhere disinterested in our lives. He isn't waiting to punish us when we get it wrong. He gave me a lesson in repentance I will never forget and I never felt one iota of condemnation from Him. He is a good God.

3 Sanctification

Sanctify them through thy truth: Thy word is truth.   (John 17:17)

Sanctify means to set apart for sacred use: to make holy: to make pure. If we are clean, God can pour His power into us. He can use us. If our eyes are sanctified, if they are made clean, we can see.

We have to read the word and let it sanctify us. We must ask the Lord to make us clean. This is not a theory. We must give serious effort and time to sanctification.

Ask the Lord to Sanctify You

I'm going to tell you what this process looks like for me. In addition to reading the word and in addition to praying and asking God to sanctify me, I ask the Lord for His holy fire to cleanse and sanctify me.

And I will put this third into the fire, and refine them as one refines silver, and test them as gold is tested. They will call upon my name, and I will answer them. I will say, "They are my people." And they will say, "The Lord is their God." (Zechariah 13:9)

The Lord will let you see what this process can look like. I'm not saying it is always like this, but this is what I have experienced on several occasions.

At the end of the day, when everyone has gone to bed, I will stay up to pray. As I pray, I try to be led of the Lord as to what to pray for. Sometimes I ask Him to sanctify me.

When I do this, I pray the same thing with my thoughts and words also. Everything focused on the Lord sanctifying me. I picture in my mind fire falling on my head, or angels dumping buckets of fire over me as I ask the Lord to cleanse me and sanctify me. I ask Him to make me clean.

If I pursue this for a little while, the Lord allows me to experience this. Usually I will pray this way, for sanctification for a couple of hours. After two hours more or less, I have literally

71

had the Lord open my eyes to see fire fall upon me. Once there appeared behind me a pillar of fire and I kept leaning my head back into it. It was amazing.

These experiences have been life changing. To see God's involvement in my life in this way has fueled my passion for the Lord.

Actively pursue sanctification in this way and you too will be blessed in like manner. God is no respecter of persons.

Deliverance

For some reason this topic is hard for a lot of us to deal with. Many of us grew up with the teaching that demons can't bother Christians. That whole thing about, "How can an evil spirit be where the Holy Spirit is?"

Many Christians will live their whole lives bound to some sin rather than face the fact that an evil spirit is afflicting them and deal with it. There is a stigma concerning this.

If an evil spirit has access to your life in some way, as you begin to press in for your sight to be made whole, he will manifest himself in some way if he can, to thwart your efforts. Then when you stop pressing in to God, he will "recede" so that you never even know he is there. But why take chances?

Personally, I minister deliverance to myself every day. As a believer, we have authority over demons, so I use it. I bind any demon that may have gained access to my life in any way, and then I command them to leave. And they leave.

Somehow we got a strange idea that only godless people in remote parts of the world are afflicted by evil spirits, and that they are the ones who need deliverance. But the Bible makes it clear who deliverance is for.

In the story of the Canaanite woman who came to Jesus for help in Matthew chapter fifteen, Jesus tells us who deliverance is for. The woman came to the Lord saying please help me. My daughter is demon possessed and is severely tormented. Jesus answers her eventually and says this...

"...it is not meet to take the children's bread and cast it to dogs. (Matthew 15:26)

This blessing of deliverance is for us, His children.

⑤ *Iniquity*

Dealing with iniquity, is also very important if we are to walk in the spirit and *see* in the spirit.

Iniquity is that twisted thing inside us that causes us to desire to sin. It is like a root, and it must be removed if you don't want to constantly keep fighting the same battles.

Prophetess Ana Mendez Ferrell has a book on iniquity that lays it all out as to what it is and how to deal with it. I highly recommend that you read it. It will change your life.

Removing iniquity has to do with repentance. When you repent, you break a legal right of sin over your life. The root of that sin may have been passed down from generation to generation. The iniquity is the root. As you repent from *every* sin you can think of that you have ever committed, you ask the Lord to remove the iniquity that is behind the sin.

The Lord will do this. Leave nothing to chance. If you feel that something may be a sin, but probably not, repent anyway. Don't do half of the work only to leave the other half undone.

To give you an idea of the scope and thoroughness that I'm talking about, when I did this it took me three weeks of constantly asking the Holy Spirit to reveal areas of my life or acts that I needed to repent over. And to be completely honest, I don't think I'm done yet.

When you have done this, you then command all of the garbage, and all of the physical substance formed by iniquity to leave you in Jesus' name. I prayed and commanded this for my spirit, soul and body. Be prepared to possibly be sick for a couple of days as this stuff leaves you. I personally wasn't sick but I just kept spitting stuff up for a few days.

If you have nothing of the enemy in you, you will operate more freely as a spirit being who *lives* in a body. You can then enter into the deep things of God without the interference that you would otherwise face.

That would include seeing in the spirit, moving in the spirit, angelic visitations or visitations from the Lord Jesus, and access to heavenly places. Also, you will find an increase in faith, as well as an increase in the anointing you carry, to do the work that the Lord has given you, such as healing the sick and casting out devils etc.

HOW TO SEE IN THE SPIRIT

Engaging the Kingdom

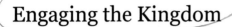

Revelation – Ask the Lord to give you the Spirit of Wisdom and Revelation. Find a quiet time that you won't be disturbed and spend some time with the Lord. I plan on at least forty-five minutes to an hour and a half.

Repentance – I know it's hard but ask the Lord to bring to mind *every* sin. Anything you could possibly repent for and do it. Do it just before you go to bed and then ask the Lord to give you further revelation about it as you sleep.

Sanctification – Find a quiet place and a quiet time to do this. Sit very, very still in a comfortable chair and close your eyes and ask the Lord to sanctify you. At first ask aloud, but after a few minutes, ask in your mind and picture the lord pouring fire on your head every time you ask. Again, spend at least forty-five minutes doing this. I mentioned earlier that I spent two hours and the result is pure joy.

Deliverance – Invest in a book such as "Pigs in the Parlor" by Frank Hammond, or another book that lists groupings of evil spirits. Read through the list and command anything that has invaded your life to leave in Jesus' name. Even if this sounds distasteful to you, just do it at least once to cover all the bases, so to speak.

Iniquity – Get Ana Mendez Ferrell's book and follow the full instructions laid out for removing iniquity.

CHAPTER SEVEN

Weapons of our Warfare

We have an arsenal. We have angelic armies. We have the blood covenant and the resurrection power of the Holy Spirit. We have not been left lacking any needed thing.

If we feel, or are, defeated in any area of our life, it's not because the Lord didn't make provision for us. Usually it's because we get lulled into an apathetic sense that we can ease up from our efforts in spiritual warfare.

Falling asleep in the middle of the battlefield is not a good idea no matter how you look at it. I know that we get weary. It's important to understand completely the dynamics of warfare.

We do not war in our own strength.

For the weapons of our warfare are not carnal, but are mighty through God to the pulling down of strongholds.
(2 Corinthians 10:4)

As you contend for your spiritual eyes to be opened, remember that you do not do it in your own strength. Graham Cooke says it this way. " *We are not fighting to victory, we are fighting from it.*"

78

I know that in theory we all understand this. But living it is another matter. As you begin to do warfare on behalf of your eyes and spiritual senses, you really must do it from a place of rest, and a place of joy.

All we are doing is enforcing a victory that Christ has already won for us. *His* authority and power are on display in our lives, not our own. As we speak *His* word, angelic armies are set in motion. The more your eyes open, the more you will see the reality of this.

...The joy of the Lord is your strength.   *(Nehemiah 8:10)*

Extreme Joy, Extreme Power

In 2010, I attended an Annual Men's Conference in northern Indiana. While there I met people of all types, from many walks of life who were called to the ministry of deliverance.

Some were very serious people and some were easygoing in nature. All were successful in their calling because we move in the authority of Christ. Not in any qualifications we might have apart from that.

During dinner, I met a young black man from a Chicago area church also there for the conference.

He began to tell me and another man at the table, of exploits that the Lord was using him for, that were extraordinary and exciting. He told these stories of rousting and defeating demons, with a big smile on his face and laughter in his voice, He had so much joy and excitement in the battle that it was in no way work for him.

And here is the point I want you to really get...I have been in the presence of great men of God. They are men that you would know. And I have never felt power coming off of a human being like I did from that young man. Frankly, it scared me a little. I have only ever felt that from angels, with the exception of only a couple of people who carried something very similar to that power.

The reason I tell you this is because I don't want you to make the same mistakes I have made. Do not strive for your spiritual sight. Know that the Lord wants you to see. Know that the Lord will not withhold any good thing from you. And do your warfare from that place of confidence in God that He has already won the victory. Do it with joy!

Prayer

Prayer will open your eyes.

The effectual fervent prayer of a righteous man availeth much. (James 5:16)

Learn how to pray from people who know how to pray.

Pray with your Whole Heart

When you pray, try to be focused on what you are praying about. In general, that is a good rule. Specific to our journey, as you pray for your eyes to open, pray with your entire being. Pray with your voice, your desire, your soul, your consciousness and with your thoughts.

Here is what it looks like. I am praying for the Lord to open my eyes.

"Lord, thank you for opening my eyes. Your word says you came to give sight to the blind and I stand in agreement with your word. I thank you that I can see! I thank you that you withhold no good thing. Thank you Jesus for applying the eye salve of Revelation 3:18. I receive my sight Lord. Thank You Lord!"

While my mouth is praying those words, in my imagination, I am watching Jesus smear eye salve on my eyes. I am seeing my eyes being opened. I am watching angels look at me realizing that I can see them now.

In my soul and emotions, I am making myself *feel* the excitement of this occasion! I become overwhelmed with the feeling of seeing the unseen!

Why? Why do I do that? Isn't that just pretending? Pastor and evangelist Mel Bond calls this praying with your whole heart. I believe it is the only way to pray. You are focused and undivided in your spirit, soul and body. This is how it's done.

How many times have you been in church singing the worship songs or listening to the message from the speaker, only to also be wondering what time church will be over today? Or seeing in your mind how long the line at the buffet is because he was a little long-winded today? You're thinking about two things.

This is why we pray with our whole heart. So we can take every thought captive unto the obedience of Christ. If you want your eyes to open, you can't be praying double minded prayers.

Intercession

This is a great truth about the kingdom, as we pray for others to get the blessings they need from the Lord, He also blesses us. He blesses us even more so than if we had only prayed for ourselves. You know the scripture...

But he that is greatest among you shall be your servant. (Matthew 23:11)

If you will spend some time praying for, blessing and lifting up others, the Lord will give you an exponential blessing. It is even more so if the person you are praying for is not worthy of that blessing. And this will open your eyes as well.

My Boss from Heck

The Lord gave me a first- hand lesson and revelation concerning this truth. It only took me three long years to finally "get it."

At one time in my life, I was given a boss who was mean, rude, ill –tempered, deceitful, and those were his good points! You can imagine!

I would go to work and he would brow beat me in front of people, threaten to fire me, find ways to make me work "off the clock", and so on. My prayer for him was "Lord please let him not suffer too much as the bus runs him over." I had no love for him. But what I failed to consider was the fact that God is not willing that *any* should perish. He loved this guy! And He wanted to save him!

One night I was in my prayer chair, asking the Lord for deliverance from this ungodly man and the Lord spoke to me. "I want you to bless him." Is what the Lord said. I wasn't really on board with that but I began anyway, "Lord bless him with salvation and bless him with deliverance, save him from hell." Not a real enthusiastic offering.

The Lord spoke to me again and said, "No, bless him as if he was your son." Well, if he was my son I would definitely pray differently. So I began. It took me a little while to really feel sincere but I blessed him every way I knew how. I blessed his life, his family, his finances and everything else I could think of. I gave him two and a half hours of my undivided prayer time.

When I was done, my spiritual eyes opened, and an angel of the Lord showed up and gave me a small gift. It was a gift that signified that I was justified now through faith in the word of the Lord. He had told me what to do. I did it in faith even though I didn't really understand why I had to do it. But God blessed me.

And I also found out that my boss no longer had any hold on my life or my emotions. The Lord had set me free. Then, on top of that, two weeks later he was fired. The Lord moved him out of my life. I think that if perhaps I had interceded for this man three years earlier I would have saved myself a lot of grief

If you want the Lord to give you the desires of your heart, intercede for others. It pleases the Lord and He will reward your obedience.

Breaking open the Spirit Realm

I was very worried one night about someone whom I love and I decided I would intercede for them. I know the song says "why worry when you can pray", but I was praying *because* I was worried. I'm just trying to be real.

I hit my knees and began to pray. Since I didn't really know what to pray for or about, I prayed in tongues. Because I did *feel* a burden, I prayed with intensity. I didn't have to try and work it up. At about the four hour mark, the burden began to lift, and as it did, the Lord transported me to the place where he was. (You will find this is not uncommon if you intercede for others.) I found myself standing in the same room with him and I could see exactly what was going on in the room, in the natural *and* in the spiritual realms. (I verified all this later with the man.)

The Lord showed me through this encounter exactly what and how He wanted me to pray for this individual. So now I could also pray with understanding as well.

The Lord Jesus was and is a servant to all. That is what a good father is. If you desire to be like Him through interceding, He will be very pleased that you sacrifice your own agenda to help others and He will really bless you.

Pressing through in Prayer

I have been guilty, too many times, of praying for the most serious of things without serious conviction.

A thirty second prayer of "Lord heal so and so" or some brief mention tacked onto another prayer. Thankfully the Lord is merciful and patient. The Lord has taught me about the incredible privilege we have to press through in prayer.

Pressing through in prayer is praying until you have a sense that something has been done. Something has been accomplished.

When you "lift up" a person or a situation in prayer, you know that sometimes the burden can actually feel almost physical. There can come a shift in the spirit realm, where you can feel that burden either lift or lessen. That is a simple explanation of pressing through in prayer. "Prayer changes things" is not some religious catch-phrase. It is a powerful truth. It is a great opportunity and privilege and an incredible weapon and tool! This is the kind of prayer that opens spiritual eyes.

Did I not Say, If You would Just Believe

Mahesh and Bonnie Chavda, evangelists and pastors of All Nations Church in Charlotte, North Carolina, know about pressing through in prayer. Mahesh received a call from day from the very distraught parents of a little girl who was dying of liver disease. The doctors had done all they could do, and their little girl had perhaps only days to live.

The parents told Mahesh that the Lord had told them to "call the General", and they knew the Lord meant Mahesh. Mahesh and Bonnie agreed, they would pray. They began to pray and the Lord Jesus joined them. Mahesh tells of how they were supernaturally transported into the girl's liver, and they ministered to every cell. Mahesh, Bonnie, and the Lord Jesus prayed for *twenty-six hours* for the girl! Yes, I said *twenty-six hours*. This is not a typo!

After twenty-six hours, the Lord told them "It is done." Mahesh then called the parents and told them "It is done." And it was! The Lord had given the girl a perfect, brand new liver. The doctors could give no medical explanation. Mahesh and Bonnie had pressed through in prayer. Learn to press through in prayer!

As you contend for your spiritual sight, sometimes you l press through. Evangelist Neville Johnson says that sometimes you may have to fast and pray to break through into the spirit, but once you do, that it's fairly easy to maintain.

Decree, Declare and Prophesy!

You should already know that words are powerful. You should know that you can shape your destiny or the destiny of those around you by the words that you speak. That is why we will be accountable for every word.

I make decrees over my family every day. I speak blessings over my family every day. I declare things from God's word over my family every day. Things like,...

... As for me and my house we will serve the Lord.

(Joshua 24:15)

No weapon formed against us shall prosper....

(Isaiah 54:17)

He has given His angels charge over us...

(Psalms 91:11)

Angels listen for God's word to perform it. And they do.

The Bible says

Thou shalt also decree a thing and it shall be established unto thee, and light shall shine upon thy ways. (Job 22:28)

There is power in your decree and in your agreement with this word of the Lord. If you decree on the authority of the Word that your eyes will open and see clearly, it will come to pass.

The Lord is not a man that He should lie, nor the son of man that He should repent. If He said it, will He not do it? (Numbers 23:19)

I really was not aware of this word or the power of this word until I heard Bobby Conner teach on it. The Lord had sent Bobby out west during a raging wildfire that had burnt up hundreds of thousands of acres with no end in sight. It was August and they were in a drought, and everything was like firewood. The Lord asked Bobby, *"How long are you going to let that go on? I want you to go and prophesy a snow storm."*

Bobby flew to Montana and went as close to the fire as the law would allow, stood on the mountain and prophesied a snowstorm to fall. He has the newspaper clipping from the following day's paper. It says, *"Surprise Snowstorm, Fires Extinguished, Job Well Done!."(WOW!)*

On the heels of Bobby Conner's testimony, One day I was asking the Lord about something very, very big I was dealing with, and the Lord reminded me of Bobby's teaching and told me to decree a thing. I said "Lord, I'm not sure I have faith for that, could I decree something small first, so you can build my faith up?" The Lord told me, "Yes, go ahead."

So, remembering Bobby's snow testimony, this was the decree I made..."In Jesus' name I decree that it will snow here today!" Now, I was in Indiana, it was August, the temperature was in the low 70s. But I really felt that if the Lord honored this decree, then I could believe for the bigger thing.

I was driving around the city all day working, but at the same time I was watching the sky closely. All morning and all afternoon I looked for the snow. I probably stopped looking for the snow about five pm or so. At about seven pm, I was kind of absent-mindedly driving along, listening to the radio. All of the sudden there were snow flurries coming down upon my truck!

It was amazing and exciting, and I was almost giddy with excitement! I watched the snow coming down for ten to fifteen seconds, and then I *said, "No!"* as in, no, I don't believe this is really happening! As soon as I said no, the snow flurries stopped! I immediately complained to the Lord about the flurries not lasting longer. And He told me that I had stopped the flurries by the word I had spoken. And then He told me to be careful of the words I speak because they have power.

That is the power of speaking God's word! If He can send a snowstorm, He can open your eyes. Decree the word of the Lord over your spiritual senses. Declare His will concerning your sight. Prophesy to your eyes! "Eyes you will see in Jesus' name!"

Engaging the Kingdom

Prayer – Pick something that you really need or you really want to pray about. Pray exactly the way I described it to you. See the prayer coming to pass in your mind and imagination. Keep your whole being engaged and of one accord. Do this at first for at least ten minutes and try to add more time as you continue. It becomes easier.

Intercession – There is someone in your life who you really have no desire to pray for. Think for a few minutes on where this person may spend eternity. Ask the Lord to give you a burden for this person. Give them one hour of the best blessing and prayer that anyone has ever prayed over them. Afterward, sit very quiet and still and ask the Lord if He wants to tell you anything, and then listen for his voice. Or, if there is someone with a great need, intercede the same way for two hours.

Decree, Declare and Prophesy! – Consider any problem or situation you have going on in your life. Decree every day ten times a day what you desire to come to pass. Do this for a week and watch God move. Declare every morning and every night just before sleep that the eyes of your heart are being enlightened. And finally, prophesy over your home. "Home, you are a Bethel and a gateway to Heaven. You are a habitation of angels. You are a place to reveal the Lord's glory!"

As you do these things, be sensitive to the spiritual atmosphere around you and in your home. See how the atmosphere changes. In all these "exercises" be aware of what is going on around you.

HOW TO SEE IN THE SPIRIT

CHAPTER EIGHT

Honor and Focus

Then the Lord answered me and said: Write the vision and make it plain on tablets, that he may run who reads it. (Habakkuk 2:2)

Journaling

One of the very first things you should do is buy a journal or a notebook of some kind. You will need this in which to record all of the things the Lord shows you as your eyes are opened. This has been a part of the process for me as well. Every little thing the Lord shows me or allows me to see, I try to enter it into the journal. By doing this, you show the Lord and yourself as well that these things have *value* to you.

Everything is everything. Every little sparkle, every flash of light, every shift in the atmosphere around you is something you should note. This includes your dreams as well. You make room for the supernatural things of God by honoring them. It is a step of faith in even buying the journal, that you believe that the Lord is going to tell you or show you something significant enough that you would record it.

As you set your journal out, you are making a statement. *"I expect something to happen."*

Another great thing about the journal, is that it keeps the vision fresh. It keeps a reminder that God just did something. I found it very surprising that many people, including myself, could have the most profound experiences, only to forget them within weeks. Anytime I start feeling sorry for myself, *"God it has been ages since you have spoken to me!"* I get my journal out and realize, ok, well maybe not ages but days instead.

You will dream more and your dreams will be more all the more significant. God will use your journal to teach you and as a way to bless others. As you intercede more for others you will find yourself having dreams about them and their situations. Your eyes will be opened as you sleep as well as when you are awake.

Keep your journal ready with a pen on top of it. If you can, write it right away while the experience is fresh.

Thankfulness

It's harder to bless people who you know are ungrateful for what you have given them. If you give someone a twenty and they can't say thanks, how much more difficult would it be to give them a thousand?

I just want you to have an understanding about being thankful for the little victories as your sight opens. Make sure that every day you thank the Lord that you can see. Thank Him for every little supernatural thing that happens. Many times as I go through my day, the Lord will show me flashes of light, sometimes it doesn't seem like much at all, but as you learn, it is sometimes hard to know exactly what is really significant.

Do not dismiss anything as, *"Well it was only this or only that."* Keep a humble heart and show honor to the "small" things and record them as well.

Exercise your Senses

Just like anything else, you get better with practice. This includes spiritual things as well. If you grew up in most evangelical churches, you might have a little trouble with this concept. Most churches teach that everything from God is sovereign and you won't or can't make a difference one way or another.

But that is not what I have found in scripture or in my personal experience. I have never had much revelation or visitation come upon me as I'm just hanging out watching TV. I've had some, but not much. But if I choose to come aside and sit at the Lord's feet I hear from the Lord. I encounter His visions and the angelic host. It's my choice.

How, you may ask? Being aware is the first step. You know the spiritual reality is right there where you can reach out and touch it. It's closer than that. Stillness is a key. You can't sense or feel or see anything if you are preoccupied with anything in the natural.

You have to take some time to do your "workout." Five minutes here and two minutes there will do nicely because it will keep you engaged more so than spending an hour and then forgetting about it.

If you look at the atmosphere around you, and study it, you can see ripples in it as surely as you can see ripples in a pond. The key is this. Don't look at the tree on the other side of the yard, look at the "empty" space between you and the tree.

I practiced this over a summer when I spent a lot of time outdoors and by the end of a couple months I could see the spiritual atmosphere, alongside the physical within minutes of looking for it. To me, it looks very similar to heat rising off of a black-top road on a hot summer day.

As I wait on the Lord, sometimes I exercise my senses as well. Focus on all of your natural senses. This is like one of the gateways. As you focus on seeing something with your eyes closed or hearing something when there are no natural sounds around, your spiritual senses become engaged.

Another key to exercising is being relaxed. If you are anxious, you will not be in faith. Don't worry or strive. God will break it open over you if you desire and honor it. He knows your heart.

Always be looking. Always be engaging your spiritual eyes. Don't feel like you have to take a break from it. How often do you take a break from your natural eyesight? You don't, as long as you have a need to see.

The Best Time for a Workout

I don't believe in coincidence anymore, so I can't say I discovered this by accident. The best time or the easiest time to see the spirit realm is late at night or very early in the morning.

Gary Oates mentioned to us at a conference in North Carolina once that early in the morning you can engage God without fighting all the clutter of the day. You haven't done anything to steal away your attention yet. You don't have a struggle like you might have say, late in the afternoon.

If you are able to lie in bed without falling asleep, a great time use your sense of sight is just before sleep when it's dark. Make sure your room is quite dark, perhaps just a nightlight if you use them, and lie still with your eyes open. This way you will be engaging spiritual sight alongside your natural sight.

In that place of "not quite dark" you'll see things much easier in the spirit. Your natural sight can't really focus because there is not enough light, and you really don't want it to anyway. In the twilight, focus on the atmosphere in the room up towards the ceiling where you won't be distracted by any furniture.

After a while, a few minutes or so, (I'd give it at least ten.) you will see very, very subtle movements of light and perhaps color. It usually isn't anything extreme at first. As you focus in a relaxed way, what you focus on will expand or become more apparent.

That is one way you exercise your sense of open sight.

Living Creatures in the House

I'm convinced that we don't have a clue as to the atmosphere in our homes. While we are hoping God *sends* an angel, there are probably ten in the living room awaiting us for prayer time.

One night past midnight, I was lying in bed and happened to open my eyes. I wasn't trying to see anything, but had a brief glance of a subtle shift of some kind to my right. I looked at it for maybe forty-five seconds or so. Suddenly it came into focus and it looked at first like a horse's head. The more I looked at it I saw that it was not that. After he knew that I was looking at him, he flew away. As he did, his body went past me and I would estimate that he was perhaps thirty feet long. He moved as if he was swimming through water.

I had no fear whatsoever, and no sense that it was anything demonic. I believe it was a living creature. I got the sense that he was there just watching over us like the angels do. Very cool!

These are the types of things that you may see as you engage your sight. Do not be in fear at all about what you may see, God gives us grace to not only deal with things as they come but to *really* enjoy the journey as well!

Waiting on God

Lead me in you truth, and teach me; for you are the God of my salvation; on you do I wait all the day. (Psalm 25:5)

This is one of my favorite things to do. And if you really love the idea of seeing, and engaging the spirit realm it will be one of your favorite things. When you wait on the Lord, you are making yourself available to Him. Whatever you want Lord, is what you are saying. My time is your time.

Some of the coolest adventures I've ever had in God, I've had while waiting on the Lord. You do not navigate these adventures alone either. The Lord has given His angels charge over you and they let you know they are around when you need them.

Angels in your Face

One thing I've found that happens quite a bit when you wait on the Lord is angels "checking you out." As I wait, eventually a shift happens and my spirit becomes aware. As this happens, my spiritual eyes open and I see what is around me. Many times angels have had their faces very close to mine as if either checking to see if I'm awake yet, or possibly pulling me into the spirit. They can do that with no problem.

Praying in the Spirit

After I think I'm done waiting on the Lord, sometimes I will get up from my chair and walk around the house praying. I will lift my hands and go all through the house praying quietly over each room. After I've done that, I go to bed. Many times after praying all through the house, I go back into the living room only to find that my body never went with me. I see my body is still in the chair and I have to go "get" my body and then go to bed.

Mission Trips in the Spirit

This adventure is from yet another time of waiting on the Lord. I had pretty much prayed, worshipped and waited all night on this occasion. (Let me make it clear that I'm not trying to impress you with the amount of time I spend. I assure you that if this was a chore, I can't guarantee that I would be doing it.) I had wrapped up my time of waiting on the Lord and was going to skip the prayer through the house thing that I do sometimes.

It was past four am, and I think I may have gotten a drink and noticed that the basement light was on. I went over to the door and called downstairs, "Anybody down there?" There was no answer. I realized that I probably just left the light on. I decided to go outside and get a breath of the morning air before heading to bed. I walked to the side door of the house and stepped outside.

When I stepped outside, I was in another place. I was literally standing in front of a church somewhere, where there were lots of people gathered around for some kind of conference that was going on. I remember thinking this has got to be the coolest thing yet! I looked across the lawn of the church and I saw a black man about my age with gray around his temples. I somehow knew that his name was Joseph. At that moment the Lord made me aware that He had put money in my pocket and I was to give it to Joseph.

I walked over to him and handed him the money and said, "This is for you." Then I turned to walk away. He yelled after me "Hey! This will buy three containers of food!" He was very excited.

Next, realizing that the Lord had transported me to do this Kingdom mission, I decided I would try to find out where I was and who this Joseph was. I figured that I could look it up on the internet when I got back home.

I saw two women talking nearby so I went to them and asked them, "What can you tell me about Joseph and his ministry?" One of the women said, "Oh you'll find out all about him, he'll be here all week!" Then she said, "But let us pray for you!" And then her and her friend laid hands on me and prayed over me. Right after that the Lord brought me back.

I then spent the next twenty minutes with waves of electricity coursing through my body. It was amazing!

Now you know why I love to wait on the Lord!

Breaking it all Down

I'm going to describe to you how I wait on the Lord, and what that whole process looks like for me. This is not a formula by any means. The Holy Spirit is in charge and He may show you a more excellent way. But this will be a good, solid jumping off point for you that I have gleaned from men of God who move in such things. **If you will do this you will see**.

Usually, if I am able to, I sometimes try to take a short nap sometime in the evening if I know I will be waiting on the Lord later. I let myself drift off for an hour or so and this helps me to avoid falling asleep later.

After everyone goes to bed and I'm pretty sure they are asleep, I go to my prayer chair downstairs. My prayer chair is a big comfortable, overstuffed chair in the living room. Sometimes I will kneel first, just to acknowledge Jesus' lordship over my life. Sometime I will stay there for a while and sometimes for only a few minutes. Then I sit in my chair and purposely try to get as comfortable as possible. It can be very distracting if you are in an uncomfortable position while you are trying to pray.

I repent of any known or unknown sins in my life. I ask the Lord to remove anything that defiles me and anything that offends Him. Sometimes I ask the Lord to send His Seraphim with coals to sanctify me.

And then I sit very, very still. I stress this because if you are thinking about all the movements that you are making, scratching your nose, adjusting your glasses or just moving too much, your focus will be divided. You are trying to engage the spirit realm and your focus will be on the natural. You don't want to divide your focus.

So now I'm comfortable and I'm sitting very still with my eyes closed. Sometimes I will picture the Lord Jesus in my mind. This is very much like if I asked you to close your eyes and "see" what your house looks like. Or, sometimes I will think about a scripture or even a previous vision that the Lord has shown me.

Now I wait. I wait with the expectation that the Lord will speak to me or manifest Himself to me in some way. I "listen" as if I am on guard and I have to be diligent to hear any strange sounds no matter how faint they may be. In other words I actively listen. I allow my senses to notice any strange or any different sensations I may feel.

Even though my eyes are closed, I "look" to see any flicker of light or color or anything at all different from what you would normally see with your eyes closed.

As I "look" and "listen", when I know that there are no natural sights or sounds to see or hear, a shift begins to take place. My spirit takes over and my spiritual senses become engaged. As my spiritual senses become engaged, I see what is around me in that realm. That is why it will be normal for you to see the angels who minister with you and for you when you wait on the Lord. They are always around. Always. They may not be interacting with you when you see them. They may be doing other things, but you will see them because your eyes will be open.

I just want to take a minute to remind you that as believers we have a right to seek and expect for the Lord to visit with us or appear to us or embrace anything else He wants to do.

Whoever has my commandments and keeps them, he it is who loves me, and he who loves me will be loved by my Father, and I will love him and manifest myself to him (John 14:21

Imagination

Imagination has gotten a bad rap from the church world. Any time you hear about it you seem to get the warnings from people who want to tell you how "new age" people use the imagination, or how the Bible says we are to *cast down imaginations,* while conveniently forgetting to quote the rest of the verse.

Imagination is a gift from God. Adam had to use his imagination to name all the animals in the garden. One can use the imagination for good or for evil. The imagination just needs to be sanctified so that it fulfills God's purpose.

One of the major hang-ups I had with this word was that from childhood on I was taught that imagined meant "not real" or "pretend." *Just* your imagination was always a phrase to dismiss imagination as not real or not important. So when I began to be taught from men of God that the imagination was a very powerful key or doorway into the spirit, I had a lot of hurdles to jump over. How could pretending something be the same as it really happening? I don't want to *pretend* to see angels. I want to really see them!

What we first have to realize is that thought is communication in the spirit realm. When you talk to an angel, or even to a demon, (to rebuke him) you never even have to open your mouth. When you pray you don't have to speak either. The Lord not only hears prayers that you think, but can also feel the emotion with which you pray. You can pray just by imagining. If you imagine yourself bowing at Jesus' feet in worship, then you have just worshipped Him, and He accepts that as true worship.

But I say unto you, that whosoever looketh on a woman to lust after her hath committed adultery with her already in his heart. (Matthew 5:28)

Imagination is reality to the Lord.

Use your imagination in every part of your Christian walk. Use it in prayer, and in worship. Use it while waiting on the Lord, or when praying for the sick. Practice using your imagination by putting yourself into biblical scenes or imagine the visions that John or Ezekiel describe as if they are happening to you. What will happen is that you will find yourself being "pulled" into these visionary experiences. The doorway is your imagination.

More Mission Trips

During times of waiting, I began to imagine myself being taken to third world countries to pray for the sick. I would "fly" there and pray for a few sick folks and then "fly" back. I would also tell the Lord, "Lord I am willing to do this if you want me to." It wasn't too long after that, that the Lord began using me in that way. There is Biblical precedent for this, and it is happening to believers around the world. There is Bruce Allen, Ian Clayton and Mahesh Chavda to name but a few. Let's add your name to that list!

Engaging the Kingdom

Journaling – Get your journal started. Let your first entry be a prayer to the Lord that He Himself would fill that journal with mighty exploits that give Him glory!

Exercise your Senses – Pick the hour that will best work for you, morning or night, and spend ten to fifteen minutes looking on the unseen. Also, take a few minutes to also do this as you wait on the Lord.

Waiting on God – This one is your *key to supernatural adventures in God.* Do not neglect this. You will not be disappointed. Do the things I described for you and try to wait on the Lord for forty-five minutes to an hour and a half. If you are able to spend more time with the Lord, maybe on a day when you don't have to get up early the next day, go a little longer!

Imagination – Pick out some scriptures that you really love, and imagine yourself as being there. Imagine the sights, sounds, smells, feelings and emotions. Try to make a promise to yourself that you will do this at least twice a week until it starts to transport into the experience.

- Also, Lyn Packer has an excellent book that would be extremely helpful to you here as well and in general, concerning spiritual sight. It's called...
  " Visions, Visitations, and the Voice of God"

HOW TO SEE IN THE SPIRIT

CHAPTER NINE

Feeding your Spirit

It is the spirit that quickeneth; The flesh profiteth nothing; The words that I speak unto you, they are spirit and they are life. (John 6:63)

There are the things that should be more obvious, like prayer and Bible study. And other things like church attendance and fellowship as well. These things are a given for Christian life in general, as well as for opening your spiritual eyes.

In my own journey, there were several other things that I considered very significant in causing my eyes to open. I'm going to start with perhaps one of the most important things.

Testimonies

In an atmosphere of testimonies of God's greatness, anything can happen. Bill Johnson of Bethel Church in Redding, CA, says that the root word of testimony means "to do again." Testimonies will inspire you to believe for the things you desire. God is no respecter of persons, what He does for another He will do for you.

Fellowship with people who love Testimonies

My wife Gordana, has a friend who we get together with for fellowship. As we talk about the greatness of God, and share testimonies of what we have seen and heard, her face gets covered in gold sparkles. It's one of the coolest things! The Lord confirms His word with signs and wonders.

Sharing and repeating testimonies of miracles and signs and wonders that you are aware of or have experienced will cause that to come upon your life as well. Honor the things that God has done and He will manifest it in your life as well. If you don't honor it, He won't force it upon you.

Her friend also told us about an amazing television program that presents weekly programs highlighting incredible miracles, signs and wonders that God is doing upon the earth *today!*

It's Supernatural

Evangelist, Creator and host of the television program, It's Supernatural, Sid Roth is fulfilling the mandate of the Lord to propel the willing into the supernatural things of God. I don't recall which program was the first one I watched, but my wife and I have not missed very many in the past four years.

I can honestly say that watching and *participating* with this program has taken our family into the most incredible things we have ever experienced! Again, it's the power of a testimony! Watching these programs fueled both my hunger and my faith. Everyone on the programs, and Sid really makes this clear, emphasizes that this is for *everyone!* This is not just for the "superstar" minister or evangelist.

All this is for us! Spiritual sight and senses, signs and wonders, healings and miracles are supposed to be normal in the life of a believer.

This program is food for your spirit man. It is my advice that you consume all the "bread" available from the archived programs as well. Go through each and every one. Fill yourself on testimonies of the power of God. Learn from those who see openly in the spirit. Pray *all* the prayers of dedication and impartation along with the guests. The key is that you are not watching the program as if it were entertainment, but as a source to feed your spirit man.

Encounter with the Lord

"Really Mike, how life-changing can a television program really be?" I'm glad you asked. While watching Sid interview Dr. Bruce Allen, a man the Lord is using to teach people how to move around the earth supernaturally for the cause of the Kingdom, I learned one key thing that I immediately "tried." Bruce talked about sitting quietly, waiting on the Lord with your eyes closed, and looking to see what the Lord shows you. He said that you should expect the Lord to show you something.

The next morning I had a little time, so I did as he instructed. After about forty minutes, I became aware that I was moving somewhere at a high rate of speed yet also sitting still at the same time. It freaked me out. I got up, walked around for a few minutes and then repented of my fear. I sat back down and did it again. This time after twenty minutes, I again was aware that I was sitting in my home in complete silence, yet I was also hearing incredible sounds at the same time. I again freaked out then I repented. I wasn't use to experiencing two realities.

The third time I did it nothing happened. I thought *"Well I blew it. God gave me a chance and I messed it up."* I lay down on the bed and told the Lord how sorry I was that I had let fear take what He had so freely given me. What happened next was beyond what I could have hoped for.

Immediately I was caught up into the stars. I flew to the highest places you could imagine, with no fear whatsoever. Then I descended into the ocean and got to see the wonders there. As I stood there at the bottom of the ocean the Lord Jesus spoke to me. It's the only time so far, I have literally heard his actual voice. He said *"See, I'm with you even to the depths of the ocean."* The Lord himself had taken me into Psalm 139.

Where can I go from your spirit? Where can I flee from your presence? If I go up to the Heavens, you are there; If I make my bed in the depths you are there. (Psalm 139:7,8)

Watch It's Supernatural!

2 *The Atmosphere of the Supernatural*

Being around people who see in the spirit or those who manifest any spiritual gift, it causes that gift to be manifested in your own life. You should cultivate friendships with people of like mind. (spirit) You should go to conferences and classes where the power of the Lord is honored. Get close to the people who move in the gifts that you desire for your own life. If you go to a conference, get close to the speaker. If they have a prayer line, get in it. If they don't have a prayer line, politely ask them to lay hands on you anyway. I have found that most people who really move in God's power are very gracious.

Angelic Shield

In 2010, I went to a conference in Ohio hosted by Prophetic Psalmist, John Belt and his wife Brandi. One of the speakers was Evangelist/Pastor Ryan Wyatt. He was teaching on being naturally supernatural. He was teaching on seeing in the spirit realm. He explained the way he does it and how to engage that in your own life. It was a great time. After the first day, I went to the hotel to sleep. On awakening the next morning, I opened my eyes and right there next to my head was a round, semi-transparent shield hanging in mid-air! After a few seconds it faded from sight. I have seen this type of thing happen over and over. Just being in that atmosphere opens your eyes to that realm.

Life Altering Conference

The kingdom Foundations conference conducted by Randy Clark, Bill Johnson, Will Hart, Tom Jones and Steve Swanson, at Dayspring Church in Springfield Missouri in November of 2011 was probably the most life altering conference we have been to, to date.

There were a thousand people, from all over the country, hungry for the deep things of God. The atmosphere was thick and tangible. Great things were happening. The Lord had graciously given me a word of knowledge that I got to share, and I also had a prophetic dream the first night there. It was very nice.

On the second day of the conference, I believe, 11/11/11, my wife Gordana was crying out, during a time of prayer and worship and impartation. Our lives have never been the same.

My wife Gordana had been raised in a church that doctrinally accepted things like miracles and tongues but it was not anywhere in evidence in the church body. After she had seen up close, God do amazing things, she had a hunger for it and for living in the reality of it. But after a couple years of asking the Lord to give her an experiential reality of it, and not seeing it come to pass, she was weary. She was wrestling with the idea of giving up the pursuit of God, and just living a good, religious life. That was the place she was in spiritually when we went to the conference in Missouri.

During the time of prayer and impartation, she was crying out to the Lord. "Lord you can't let me go back home the same. You have to do something." She was weeping and travailing and it was heartbreaking to watch. But, God heard her prayer.

To be honest, I can't recall the exact order of who prayed when, but I know that both Randy Clark and Will Hart laid hands on her and prayed a prayer of impartation. All of the sudden, Gordana started shaking violently side to side, moving in ways that appeared not to be humanly possible. This continued the first day for about two hours, then also the following days about two to three hours per day. She could not speak or walk. She had virtually no control over her body. (I later found out that this is a common thing among intercessors.)

I found out after she could talk, that an angel had come and stuck his hand into her chest and shook her. There are actually two angels involved in this and they still come to this day. She sees them on a regular basis. Our lives have never been the same since. They don't ask us when it might be convenient that they show up. They serve God's agenda. I could write an entire book just on this one event and what has come from it.

The conference atmosphere is one you should drink deep from. Don't listen to naysayers who tell you that you are chasing after a new word, or a sign and wonder. I've had some of my closest friends tell me that I shouldn't go here and there to receive from God. That God will give me everything I need without going anywhere. If you are hungry for God, go wherever you have to. If you are hungry to see, get around the people who already do. I like how Pastor Bill Johnson addresses this subject.

"Everyone says you shouldn't follow after signs and wonders. I say follow them until they start following you!"

Impartations

This is another big resource to draw upon from the Lord. There are people who spend incredible amounts of time in God's presence. These people have tangible power flowing in , around and through them. They, by God's power, can break chains off of you or bring down veils that would hinder you. If you have the opportunity and any of these people come to within a couple hundred miles of where you are, go see them. Let them impart to you. And when you stand before them, *draw* on their gift!

Pack your Bags we're going to Brazil!

Pastor/Evangelist Michael Kaylor was told by many well meaning people not to go to Brazil with Randy Clark, for God to touch Him. That God could do it right where he was. Michael said, "I know He can, but he's not. So I'm going to Brazil!" It was a very good choice. God moved big time. After a prayer of impartation, Michael's eyes were opened to the angelic realm, extra angels were assigned to his ministry, and he was baptized in fire several times! He moves in a powerful anointing now that he didn't have before. You can read all about it in his book, "The Adventure of Supernatural Discovery."

School of the Seers

Author/Evangelist Jonathon Welton went to a meeting and was prophesied over by Prophet/Evangelist Dennis Cramer. After the prophetic word was given to him that his eyes would be open even more than he would like them to be, his eyes were opened. They were so opened that he was freaked out by the fact that he could continually see in the spirit. He could see angels, demons, and a lot of stuff he had no understanding for! The Holy Spirit taught him. I know that he is glad now that he went.

Why didn't you Drink?

A few years ago I attended a conference where Prophet Bob Jones taught and ministered. Bob spoke a word that people should come up who felt that they were to be used in ministry but that satan had stolen opportunities from them. The Holy Spirit prompted me to go up. Bob laid his hands on both sides of my head and prayed, broke curses and prophesied over me for two minutes! When I got back to my seat the Lord told me this,

"My servant had his hands on your head for a full two minutes. Why didn't you draw from him?" I didn't have a good excuse. For some reason I went up with the attitude that whatever God wanted to do, He would do. I would receive it. That is not the attitude God likes. He wants us to be hungry. He wants us to contend for His presence. He wants us to draw from Him and drink from His provision. Keep that in mind as those who possess the gift you desire, pray over you.

People can only impart what they possess. Many have pressed through and broken chains and pulled down strongholds that block spiritual sight. When they pray for others they carry an anointing to bring that same thing to manifest in others. Find out who walks in clear spiritual sight and ask them to pray and impart to you. There are many people right now who God has commissioned to teach and impart the supernatural gifts for the end time harvest about to take place.

Get in Line and be prepared to receive!

Atmosphere in your Home

The atmosphere in your home is another way to feed your spirit. If your Home is filled with the atmosphere of Heaven it will break down barriers that will affect the entire family and everyone who enters your home.

We set the atmosphere through all the things we've talked about. We set them through prayer and worship, praise and testimonies. The reading of the word is another way we set the atmosphere. We apply those things to the atmosphere of our homes.

Praise

For about a two year period, we played worship music in our home twenty –four hours a day, and seven days a week. In addition, we read the Bible aloud, we also sang praises and worshipped. What difference could this make? For starters, even people who aren't following the Lord have seen angels in our house. A friend of my son's stayed the night one night and told us the next day that we have "ghosts" in our house. I told him that that's not possible. He said that we do have ghosts because he saw them walking around in the basement. I again told him that we couldn't have ghosts because the angels in our home would never allow it. He saw the angels, and because he had no frame of reference, he thought that they were ghosts, and was afraid.

One night my cousin whom we hadn't seen for a long time came over and spent the night. The next morning he told me "You're not going to believe this." I said "Try me." He said "Last night I woke up in the middle of the night and I saw this being standing over me looking at me." I asked him if he was scared at this and he told that he was completely at peace and rolled over and went back to sleep. *He shall give His angels charge over thee...*

Full and Overflowing

If you want your home to be a place where you see angels and even strangers feel the presence of God, you have to make it so. Anoint your home with oil. Anoint every room and every doorway. Anoint your property. Prophesy over your home. Make your "sanctuary" a place where you can't help but see the unseen. Make it a place where there is so much spiritual activity going on it overwhelms the atmosphere.

Here is the type of prayer that I pray over my house.

"Father in Heaven, I call upon the resources of Heaven. I call upon the angelic armies to minister in our household. Let the angels of the Lord manifest their presence and their power openly in our home. Father let the saints and the prophets, the men in white linen, the living creatures and the cloud of witnesses minister your will to our household. Let your light and your glory fill this place to overflowing in Jesus' name."

Teachings

In the past you wouldn't have near the resources that we have today in all things prophetic and supernatural. With CDs and MP3s and books and e-books, YouTube and websites, we can learn things from every corner of the earth from the most anointed people on the earth.

CDs and MP3s and Podcasts

In today's busy world, these resources work out great to take advantage of times like driving or doing chores or working around the house. Listening to scriptures everyday is a great way to go through the Bible. Driving to work is a great time to sing along with worship music and driving home a great time to listen to teachings from your favorite ministers. I also like to listen to worship on MP3 with ear buds as I'm falling asleep. It's a great way to pave the way for revelation from Heaven. There are also podcasts that you should take advantage of from places like "The Company of Burning Hearts", "The Glory Company", and "Chiswick Christian Center."

Television, DVDs, and You Tube Programs

You may not be able to attend the conference on the opposite coast, but chances are you can either get a DVD of it or see it on You Tube. There are ministries like Paul Keith Davis' "White Dove Ministries" that put out a "Webinar" to teach and equip people to walk in the supernatural things of God. Sadhu Sundar Selvaraj's "Jesus Ministries" also puts out incredible teachings on Angel TV. Bethel Church in Redding California has teaching that they offer over the web. Also Ryan Wyatt, Neville Johnson, Todd White and Voice of the Light Ministries also put out incredible teachings, very many of them are at no cost.

Books

My favorite source of gleaning teaching! Get a marker and a pen, and study the books of people to whom God has given revelation. Many have scripture references to verify the teachings that they present. There is an incredible amount of teaching available that you should take advantage of. Books by people that see the spirit realm, talk to the Lord face to face, and move in the things of God as a lifestyle, not an event.

I'd like to recommend just a few books that I believe have helped me in my quest to increase my spiritual sight.

Open My Eyes Lord by Gary Oates

The School of the Seers by Jonathon Welton

Fasting and Prayer by Steven Brooks

Visions, Visitations and the Voice of God by Lyn Packer

The Seer Anointing by Brenda McDonald

How to See in the Spirit World by Mel Bond

Quantum Fasting by Emerson Ferrell

Eyes That See by Patricia King

Iniquity by Ana Mendez Ferrell

Gazing into Glory by Dr. Bruce Allen

Engaging the Kingdom

Testimonies – Get in a place where you can hear or share testimonies of the supernatural things of God. If that's not possible, write down some miracles you've heard about or are aware of and meditate on them.

The Atmosphere of the Supernatural – Plan to attend a conference or a meeting or church service where the supernatural things of God are in evidence. Make it a point to fully engage with everything available.

Impartations – Do a little research and find out who will be coming to your area that moves in the power of God or who has the gifts that you desire. Even if you can only go for the evening to receive an impartation, do it!

Atmosphere in your Home – Invest in an inexpensive CD player (about $20) and put it on continuous play to play worship music. Even when you are not listening to it, keep it playing very low anyway. Then increase the volume when you leave the house. Sometimes not everyone is on the same page concerning this. Don't blast the music at a level to make others feel uncomfortable. You don't want people to continually *want* to turn it down or off.

Teachings – Get a book if you like to read, or a CD, or MP3 if you like to listen, but get a steady diet of teachings from those who are where you want to be. Do the work and you will also receive what they have received. God is no respecter of persons.

CHAPTER TEN

Extreme Measures

(For Extreme Times)

Things that the church nowadays, would consider to be extreme, were "par for the course" so to speak, in the early church. The early church experienced visions and visitations. They had a culture of the miraculous that propelled the Gospel forth. It was all about the Lord. When the Lord gave instructions to the disciples to teach others the same things that they had been taught, He wasn't just talking about doctrine. These guys *saw* both realms, *lived* in both realms, moved in that power, and were expected to teach others to do the same.

Prayer is reaching out after the unseen; fasting is letting go of all that is seen and temporal. Fasting helps express, deepen and confirm the resolution that we are ready to sacrifice anything, even ourselves, to attain what we seek for the Kingdom of God.
Andrew Murray

The miracle workers and mystics of the past two thousand years were also people who were given to a life that was centered on God. They were" all in" with no plan b. When you read the accounts of these who saw the Lord, spoke and worked with the angels, performed miracles and signs and wonders, it's hard to even imagine that we're supposed to be part of the same family.

In our modern age, there are also those who live in both realms. They see the unseen as surely as they see the "seen." For every story they tell you of angelic visitations, there are a *thousand* more that they didn't tell. During meetings, they don't point out that they can see everything going on in the spirit because they don't want us to be distracted. But they do teach us to be like them. They openly share the sure ways to see in the spirit, and to move in the spirit. I have presented those ways in this book. Now I'm going to explain to you why *they* see so completely and clearly. What it is that allows them continuous access to the spirit realm.

Fasting

With the exception of Pastor Jentezen Franklin, I don't hear many messages on fasting these days. It is difficult to crucify the flesh, so it's not a real popular subject. If it were easy, we would do it. Fasting breaks the rule of our flesh over our spirit. Fasting is a powerful way for our spirit man to take his rightful place and his rightful authority over our beings. It brings our soul and body under subjection. When this happens, the spirit is free to engage spiritual things more fully and more easily. We forget sometimes that Jesus did not tell us, "*if*" you fast..., He told us *when* you fast.

Moreover when ye fast, be not as the hypocrites, of a sad countenance; for they disfigure their faces, that they unto men to fast. Verily I say unto you, they have their reward. (Matthew 6:16)

123

The things that hold us back are the fleshly things, the things of the soul. When we deny the flesh, the reward is exponential.

In my opinion, fasting is a lifestyle for every disciple. Fasting transformed my thoughts and has become my doorway into the spirit realm.

The physical changes in your body will reflect the spiritual transition that has begun. Moreover, if you establish fasting as a lifestyle, the heavens will remain open in your life and mind.
L. Emerson Ferrell-Author of Quantum Fasting

How long should I fast?

Even fasting one meal makes a great impact. More than you might think. There are people who make a promise to fast a meal every Friday or every Wednesday. Others fast a meal strictly to give up that time to pray or read the Word. (That's a good thing.) I usually fast from one meal to three days, depending on why I'm fasting. If I fast longer, it's because I'm led to do it, and I ask the Lord for grace to do it.

Thirteen Day Fast

Last year I was led to go on a two week fast for someone who was dying of a disease. I didn't really *feel* anything or see anything as I fasted. I just continued by faith. On the thirteenth day, late in the afternoon, I felt I heard the Lord say, "You can eat something now." I asked the Lord if He was sure. (I know He was sure, I just wasn't sure if it was Him speaking) He said yes. So I did. Later that evening, my spiritual eyes opened. I was taken to a "region of captivity", (like I talked about earlier) where I encountered the soul of the one who was sick and dying.

In the spirit, I could see the condition of the person's soul, and a cause that was making them ill. The Lord led me to ask the spirit's name, and he told me his name. Then the Lord had me rebuke the spirit and command it to leave. When I did this, the spirit immediately came out. He was very angry, but obeyed anyway. Then the Lord brought me back home. Two weeks later, I found out that the person who had been previously given only a couple of months to live, had just been given a clean bill of health! Fasting had not only opened my eyes, but also gave me the opportunity to be used of the Lord. You can't put a price on that.

I mentioned that sometimes I'm led by the Lord before I fast. You cannot live a fasted life that way though. Fast even without being led, even if it's only a meal, or a day.

If you say "I will fast when God lays it on my heart", you never will. You are too cold and indifferent to take the yoke upon you.
D. L. Moody

When you fast with a righteous cause in mind, you make strides in the spirit realm more than you could ever know. Kevin Basconi, Evangelist and Author, sees the angels that minister with him on an ongoing basis. They hang out at his house and seem to be quite comfortable being there. They engage with him and he with them. But the Lord gave him an important key early on about entering in to this reality of the spirit realm. The Lord told Kevin, *"Read and rest, fast and pray."* Kevin spent a *season*, so to speak, reading the word, resting for a while, and fasting and praying. Kevin made sure to share this in his series of books 'Dancing with Angels", so we could benefit from the Lord's instruction as well.

125

Modern Day Examples

David Hogan

Missionary/Evangelist David Hogan *and* his ministry team fast every other day as a rule. When he inquires of the Lord he fasts longer, often mentioning forty day fasts. Once, when under demonic attack, his son lost his sight and hearing. David says he fasted five days with no food or water. He told the Lord, *"This is NOT happening to my family."* On the fifth day God spoke and told him what to do, and his son was restored.

Mahesh Chavda

Pastor/Evangelist Mahesh Chavda was working in a state home for the mentally handicapped and was taking care of a boy who continually beat himself in the face. Mahesh asked the Lord, *"What's the answer for little Stevie?"* The Lord told him *"This kind goes not out but by prayer and fasting."* So Mahesh began his fast, he had fasted fourteen days with no food, the first three of those days with no water, and the Lord told him now he could go pray. Mahesh prayed, the boy was supernaturally flung fifteen feet through the air, and completely set free from his affliction. There is extreme power in extreme actions when they are born of God.

Many in the Prophetic "Camp" begin their year in fasting and prayer because it causes them to *see* more clearly.

If you have longed to interact with the angels, fasting will remove the veil and expose you to their participation in your life. L. Emerson Ferrell

Fasting is what prepares you for a new anointing...There is a prophetic release that occurs in a church or an individual who fasts continually for forty days. Jentezen Franklin

2 Extreme Prayer

I touched on this in pressing through in prayer earlier. This would be kind of like that but with exponential increase. If you are willing to pray until you see the breakthrough, you will see the breakthrough. The power of prayer is something that is hard to comprehend without divine understanding. We don't realize the power and authority that we have been given and what it can accomplish.

Pray Until You See

Kevin Basconi was told by the Lord to pray in tongues all the way to the conference he was going to attend in Canada. Kevin tells of this account in volume one, of "Dancing with Angels." He says that he prayed all the way, eighteen hours of praying in tongues non-stop. Kevin tells of being in the meeting when his eyes opened fully and completely to the spirit realm. He watched as a portal opened up in the atmosphere above him and angels came through to minister to the attendees. Not long after, the Lord Jesus himself came and ministered to another young man and to Kevin as well! This testimony alone was enough to inspire me to pray extreme! Does anybody else want to see Jesus?!

I have heard many testimonies of the church in the far-east, of how they pray and worship. Some churches are meeting every morning at four am to worship for two hours before they start the day! That's *normal* to them. *Extreme is normal to them!*

127

In his book "Baptized by Blazing Fire" Pastor Yong Doo Kim tells of ongoing *all night* prayer and warfare vigils where the "ordinary" members of the church have their eyes opened and see who and what they are warring against. Awesome!

The orders of monks in the early church, who were devoted to prayer, use to lash themselves to support beams and posts so as to keep themselves upright in a standing position so they could pray all night without falling asleep. William Branham who moved in tremendous spiritual power and gifts, would go to a place of seclusion, such as a cave, to pray and seek God for days *until* the angel of the Lord showed up!

John G. Lake, who had one of the most astounding healing ministries of the past century, would pray for *hours or days* to see the sick healed! Whatever it took! His Healing Rooms in Spokan, Washington witnessed over one hundred thousand DOCUMENTED healings in the early nineteen hundreds. Here is an account he gives of praying for a man who was dying in the hospital.

"I prayed for him unceasingly for sixteen hours without result. One of my ministers also came to pray for him in the power of God. The man's daughters begged me to let them give him morphine and let him die."

"Presently, as I stood there, and watched the awful convulsions, particularly in his old, bare feet that were sticking out at the bottom of the bed, this (verse) came to mind"...Himself took our infirmities..."(Matthew 8:17) And I reached out and got hold of them (his feet) and held them as if in a grip of iron, and that thing that is too deep for any form of expression we know,

h in my soul, and in a single moment I saw him lay
d of God.   John G. Lake

If you will pray like these men do, you will see with open eyes

(3) *Combining the Two*

The power of prayer and fasting together cannot be over emphasized. Giving up the desire of your body to eat and then also giving up the desires of your soul (your agenda) so that you can pray, will overcome any and every obstacle.

By fasting and praying together, we can overcome every hindrance, obstruction, and mountain that blocks the way between us and our corporate destiny and calling in Christ! Victory is only found in the realm of the spirit, and that is why the devil takes every opportunity to divert us from the   mode of prayer and fasting back into the natural mode.
Mahesh Chavda

Men and women like Mahesh and Bonnie Chavda, David Hogan, John G. Lake, Kathryn Kuhlman, Kevin Basconi, Jeff Jansen, Heidi Baker, Gary and Kathi Oates, and others who have, or do see in the spirit, lives lifestyles of prayer and fasting. They walk with angels. They see the Lord and hear his voice. If we can take a lesson from them, we will also!

Engaging the Kingdom

Fasting – Make a commitment to fast at least one meal, twice *a* week. Also, pick a day when you won't be expected to eat, and fast the day. If that seems daunting at all, then fast from desserts or breads for a day. God will honor that. He is training us. He is our helper. As your experience with fasting deepens, then you can fast a full day, then three days, then seven. If you have medical issues, be smart and don't make yourself ill. As your eyes are opened to the supernatural, your fasting will be motivated by the incredible experiences the lord gives you.

Extreme Prayer – Pick something or someone you are passionate about, and go *double* the distance you have prayed before. If you've prayed an hour, go two, if two, go four. Get up and pray during the watch of the night. The supernatural realm seems to be more accessible during the night watch. If you have a day or can take a day and focus on prayer, try praying in tongues for eight hours. Don't strain for it. Pray all day but don't let it be work. Work gets tedious too fast. Keep joy in your prayer front and center. At the end of your prayer, always try to sit in stillness for at least ten minutes to really feel God's presence and let Him speak to you.

- Make sure and keep journal entries for your times of prayer and fasting. It will be a great benefit as you look and see what works for you and what doesn't.

HOW TO SEE IN THE SPIRIT

CHAPTER ELEVEN

My Personal Journey

Over the past four or five years my personal journey has changed. I don't spin my wheels as much in my pursuit and relationship with God. I no longer focus on "not" committing sins. That is one thing the Lord showed me early on. If you focus on not committing the sin, you are still focused on the sin. If I feel tempted in any type of sin, or even if I don't, my focus turns to Christ. Any thought that would offend the Lord is driven out and I imagine Him standing right there with me as if He can see my thoughts, because He can.

I try to practice the presence of the Lord in an ongoing manner, no matter where I am or what I'm doing. If you stay connected to that realm it remains open to you. I learned that, from waiting on the Lord and going back through my journals. The more you stay engaged with the realm of the spirit, the more it manifests around you and to you.

That's why I love to pray as much as I do. Sometimes friends think you may be "overdoing it" but that's only because they have no frame of reference for it. A friend texted me this week and told me that I would rather wait on God than sleep. Well, I can't deny that.

If I think I might wait on the Lord in the night, I take a short nap if I can. After everyone goes to sleep, I try to stay up for a little and pray in the silence and stillness of the house. I try to always be aware that the angels of the Lord are constantly around us, even when I'm praying in my prayer chair before bed.

Sometimes prayer time goes a little long and I find it's close to morning. Let me again mention that this life of constantly engaging the Lord is not in any sense a chore. Once the Lord has opened your eyes or brought you into things of the Kingdom or sent angels to minister to you or encourage you, there is nothing that compares to that in this natural world. I would gladly "sacrifice" four hours of my time in prayer to be positioned for an angel to come deliver a scripture to me or feel the presence of the Lord upon me. You have to experience it to understand it.

As I looked at my own life to determine how to increase the presence of the Lord, and how to see more clearly into the spirit realm, I read through my journals again. There are clear indicators that show me why sometimes I see incredible things in the spirit realm and sometimes I see nothing. The answer is time. Time invested in spiritual things brings a harvest of spiritual things. The more I seek God, the more I find Him. The more I pray for miracles, the more I experience them. The more I look, the more I see.

The Family

A great benefit of spending a lot of time in God's presence a, is that His presence also surrounds your atmosphere, i.e. your family. Since we have begun this journey several years ago by purposely positioning ourselves before the Lord, our house has become a supernatural atmosphere. People feel peace here and have told us so. I won't go into depth about all the experiences of my family members, but all of them have seen and interacted with angels. Angels have spoken to my children and given them advice, prayed for them, and given them warnings. They have also seen the demonic and driven it out of our home or their circumstances. They have felt God's presence in real and tangible ways. Jesus has manifested Himself to them. They have experienced the supernatural signs and wonders of the Kingdom first hand. I am very excited for this because I always told the Lord from day one, *"You have to bring my whole family along on this journey."*

Because of the incredible joy I've found, I've tried to bring friends and other loved ones with me. Some pursue it, some don't. An angel that was assigned to our family years ago when my parents were missionaries told me recently, *"I would have loved to have had more people to help and watch over in ministry, but people have free will. They get to choose."*, Yes, we get to choose. And I choose the path less ordinary. I choose the excitement and adventure of a Kingdom life, a life lived in God. And wherever He takes me, I am willing to go.

Journal Entries

I mentioned my journal, so I wanted to include a few journal entries to give you a real accurate accounting of how time invested in the things of the spirit can open that realm around you.

- Fri. 3 Jun 2011 3:30-4 am Worshipped on my knees by my bedside. It's a little difficult because I have to be quiet.

4-5 am Prayed in tongues and prayed for Angie (my daughter) in my mind. Somewhere between 5 and 5:30 am, I fell asleep and woke up in the spirit to see someone looking at me close-up. An angel. He looked a lot like me but with longer hair. I have a feeling he kind of pulled me into the spirit. I feel the Lord is training me.

- Wed 8 Jun 2011 1:20 am The dog woke me up. 1:25-2:20 am Worshipped the Lord. 2:20-3:20 I did warfare over the family and made Holy decrees according to Job 22:28 3:20 am went upstairs. 3:20-4:05 Worshipped on floor. 4:05-6:50 had random dreams/ Wed. afternoon-I was at the stoplight at 9th and Keystone and saw a ball of yellowish light traveling from west to east across the intersection.

- Sun 4 Jul 2011 12-2 am Prayed and fell asleep by dining room table on floor.

- Fri 15 Jul 2011 11 pm – 3:15 am Prayed over family, especially Matt and Angie. (my kids) I went to bed. Sat 16 6:20 got up. 7-8:15 I did warfare over family. I sat quietly in my prayer chair afterwards and the Lord opened my eyes. I saw the veils again and this time I watched one pretty much disintegrate.

- Thurs 3 Nov 2011 3:30 – 5 am Prayed in prayer chair. Waited on the Lord. At 5 am went to bed and was pulled into the spirit so I got back up and knelt by my bed to pray. I was then taken in the spirit to a retirement home into a woman's room. The Lord showed me that the attendant had taken a piece of the woman's clock that her husband had given her, and hidden it, to aggravate her. He showed me where it was and had me fix the clock. Then He took me to the woman's dresser so I could see a picture of her and know who she was.

- **11-11-11** Today at the impartation service w/ Randy Clark, the power of God came upon Gordana. The Lord put His hand in her chest and was shaking her for 2 hours! Gordana was undone!

- **Sun 12 Feb 2012** 2:18- 5 am Prayed for family. Did warfare for children. Had lots of dreams.

- **Mon 13 Feb 2012** I went to bed about 11 pm. Prayed for 10 minutes. Meant to pray later, but never did.

- **Fri 22 Mar 2012** I just came off a 3 day fast. I've been spending about 2 and a half, hours a day in prayer and waiting on the Lord. Tues. when I finished, I looked at the clock and it was 4:44 am. Anyway, I was laying in bed sleeping when all of the sudden I heard someone whisper my name... "Mike, Mike!" I knew there was no reason for a strange man to be in our bedroom, so I got an adrenaline rush and sprang out of bed to confront him. It was an angel! He had brought a basket with bread in it for me. He was very nice and big and powerful, and he seemed to have a great sense of humor. He told me a little bit about his ministry.

Going back over my journal entries, I've discovered that if I spend at least a couple of hours a day in prayer, my eyes are open. If I spend less, it's kind of hit and miss. If I spend much less, my eyes being opened seem to be completely a sovereign thing.

I'm not at the place where I see all the time. Neville Johnson and Jonathon Welton both talk about what it's like to see continually in both realms and that is what I am petitioning the Lord for.

And that seems to be where the Lord is leading me, and I believe that He is leading you there as well...For such a time as this.

I really want to encourage you to do the simple but effective steps that I have presented here. If you do them, you will see in the spirit realm. There is no great "secret" or complicated task that must be performed. Once your eyes are opened, it is easier to maintain, but you will find yourself still spending lots of time in the spirit because of all the joy it brings.

Parting Words

So you see by now, that seeing in the spirit realm is simple. Anyone can see in the spirit if you *choose* to. It's a choice you have to make and then support. I heard it said a long time ago that...

" *being successful at anything is simple. Find someone who is successful in what you are pursuing, find out the price they paid to get there, and then pay that price.*"

It is my sincere desire that you realize it's worth it to pay that price.

I pray that the Lord Jesus opens your eyes more completely and clearly than you have ever dreamed. I pray that He gives you grace and strength to walk in the fullness of that gift for the Kingdom and the glory of God. I pray and impart to you all the gifts and anointing that the Lord has given me. I freely give you everything I walk in and possess in spiritual things in Jesus' name. God bless you....

Mike.

About the author

Michael Van Vlymen is an author and speaker who has a passion to relay the reality of the supernatural things of God, and teach people that everyone can walk in the supernatural. Michael was raised the son of Pastors/ Missionaries and born again at five and baptized in the Holy Spirit in his twenties. In 2009, the Lord began to teach Michael about spiritual sight and open his eyes to the spiritual realm. It is his desire to let everyone know that these gifts are not for a select few, but for all of God's children. His books and ministry try to make this very clear. Michael enjoys traveling about and sharing this joyful message along with his wife Gordana and family, and also writing the revelation that the Lord gives him.

Contact Michael at

River of Blessings International Ministries

www.riverofblessingsinternationalministries.org

email info@riverofblessingsinternationalministries.org

Other books by Michael

How to do Spiritual Warfare: Workbook (Companion workbook to the book Spiritual Warfare due out soon)

If you have ever had a problem that you have not been able to solve by natural means, spiritual warfare is available to you as a believer. This book goes step by step, to make things simple and accessible to all. Don't allow the enemy to ruin your life or the lives of those you love.

Angelic Visitations and Supernatural Encounters is a diary of living in the supernatural of God.

This book is a collection of supernatural testimonies of dreams, visitations, visions, miracles, healings and much more. It is Michael's desire that these testimonies inspire you to go for everything that the Lord has for you!

Michael books are available in multiple formats, e-books and print and may be found at or ordered from bookstores worldwide.

MICHAEL VAN VLYMEN

HOW TO SEE IN THE SPIRIT

CPSIA information can be obtained at www.ICGtesting.com
Printed in the USA
LVOW07s0324170816

500723LV00018B/450/P

9 781492 244981